THE KEY TO CLOVER

To Peter and Diana –

with love,

Laurence

July 2013

THE KEY TO CLOVER

AND OTHER ESSAYS

Lawrence Sail

Shoestring Press

Printed by imprintdigital
Upton Pyne, Exeter
www.imprintdigital.net

Typeset by types of light
typesoflight@gmail.com

Published by Shoestring Press
19 Devonshire Avenue, Beeston, Nottingham, NG9 1BS
(0115) 925 1827
www.shoestringpress.co.uk

First published 2013

Cover image: Paul Klee, Tief im Wald, 1939
Aquarell und Tempera auf ölgrundierter Leinwand, 50 x 43 cm
Kunstsammlung Nordrhein-Westfalen, Düsseldorf

ISBN 978 1 907356 70 4

CONTENTS

A sense of shape	3
Unstill life	10
Message in a bottle	16
Flights	26
Alceste and the quiet coach	32
God's ideograms	40
Kafka's singing mouse	48
Nothing to declare	54
The challenge	72
Playing it safe	76
The key to clover	82
Does Coleridge knock your socks off?	92
The triumph of occasions	104
Gnomes	113
Clot	120
The gatekeeper	125

for Elizabeth

A SENSE OF SHAPE

Sometimes school comes home. After beginning to study the Tudors with their teacher, our then eight-year old twins, Rose and Grace, were discussing over breakfast Henry VIII's regrettable habit of causing his wives to be beheaded. We progressed from cereal to toast, and from the 16th century to capital punishment in general. I explained that this involved the principle that if you kill someone you should be killed in turn. 'Your mother and I are dead against it', I said, sententiously. Rose concurred: it wouldn't work anyway, she pointed out, since if it went on long enough you would be left with one person in the world and no one to do the killing. 'Actually, being beheaded isn't so bad', Grace countered, reluctant to leave the juicy subject. And why should that be? 'Because the soul can escape to heaven through the open neck'. Surrealists, eat your hearts out.

Two entirely different mindsets at work, of course – but having in common the desire to locate a pattern into which the facts might fit. And it does seem to start young, this need to define experience in terms of sensory or abstract relationship, often with a perception of, for instance, recurrence or symmetry. And even if linguistic and cultural factors may well be as important as specifically neurological aspects of our nature, patterning seems a distinctive and almost universal feature of our human make-up. This can have its obsessive side. How porous is the border between Asperger's syndrome or certain forms of autism, and a young child's observation that, at the family table, the boys and girls are sitting at a diagonal to one another?

Language, music, mathematics, paintings – all have their schematic designs (and their rule-proving exceptions), from formal language theory to the Fibonnaci numbers to the Golden Mean, not to mention fractals. But what about the overall patterns of our experience, in the perspective of a lifetime? Old age may encourage the quest for meaning, driven by time running out and the felt need to come to terms with the gap that separates 'has been' from 'might have been'. Old age may also be an elegy for time and place gone, as in Housman's 'The Land of Lost Content':

> Into my heart an air that kills
> From yon far country blows:
> What are those blue remembered hills,
> What spires, what farms are those?
>
> That is the land of lost content,
> I see it shining plain,
> The happy highways where I went
> And cannot come again.

'An air that kills' – here the sense of shape has traced nothing better than the dead end of nostalgia. Whatever the acknowledged charms of those 'happy highways' and 'blue remembered hills', it's been downhill all the way thereafter, a steeply plunging graph of diminishment. It isn't necessarily so: though many lives might appear as a parabola that reaches its apogee in the springtime of youthful activity and energy, others might climb steadily at an upward angle, accumulating success steadily and achieving the summit in middle age or later. Yet others might assume the shape of a pyramid, with a single very clear and acute summit. Some, though, are almost shapeless, a low trace constrained by need or deprivation. The idea of a shaped life is in itself a shape, an assumption of pattern made possible by a degree of material well-being.

For the old the question may begin to loom larger, although our view of what constitutes old age has been startlingly altered over the ages by scientific and medical progress, let alone the redefinition of eligibility for a state pension. Even if time prevents a return to square one, the world no longer offers itself as pure potential, as it did for Milton's Adam and Eve turned out of Eden – 'The world was all before them, where to choose / Their place of rest'. With old age comes the tacit or overt admission that we have had our time, that the machine is more or less beginning to run down, and even Eliot's recommendation that 'old men ought to be explorers' may not prevent us from making part of the exploration a retrospect. The fact that we are fortunate enough to have reached old age may not save us from foundering on the rocks of sentimentality, or the hidden reefs of what might have been. We may need to reach for the kind of consolation announced at the conclusion of Tennyson's 'Ulysses', the belief that 'Tho' much is taken, much remains', and that despite the depredations of time and fate it is still worthwhile 'To strive, to seek, to find and not to yield.'

Shape as applied to a human life is not just narrative, but evaluative. In either mode, the temptation to edit – precisely in the interests of shape – may be irresistible, with evidence destroyed or fabricated. As a story-telling species, our skill in suggesting angles and ellipses may be honed over the years. Yet we can never completely know the shape of our own life, short of death: and then it will be set in the context of someone else's partial knowledge or imaginings. But that doesn't stop us managing our own account while we can: by suppression, by elaboration, from a need to come to terms with the random and the contingent.

The coolest examination of all this was conducted by Montaigne nearly four hundred and fifty years ago. The sentences on the walls round his library, fifty-seven in all (twenty-five of them in Greek, thirty-two in Latin, and drawn from a variety of scriptural and classical sources) are certainly indications of his perception of life's shapes. Even more so are two of the items in his first book of essays: number XIX, *Qu'il ne fault juger de nostre heur qu'après la mort* (*That we must not judge of our time until after our death*) and number XX, *Que philosopher, c'est apprendre à mourir* (*That to philosophize is to learn how to die*). The former, much the shorter piece, takes historical examples such as the death of Croesus and, from Montaigne's own time, the hapless Mary Stuart, to make the point that nothing is certain until the mortal ending. Then there is the matter of a good death, for anyone 'le dernier acte de sa comédie', on which the nature of a lasting reputation may depend: thus for Scipio a good death amounted to his rehabilitation. Nearer at hand, Montaigne quotes almost exactly, without naming him, the words of his closest friend, Etienne de la Boétie, when nearing death: 'Je remets à la mort l'essay du fruict des mes estudes. Nous verrons là si mes discours me partent de la bouche, ou du cœur.' ('I consign to Death the test of the fruit of my studies. We shall thereby soon see whether my fine words come from my mouth, or from the heart.')

It's death that takes centre stage in the next essay, but not in any morbid sense. For Montaigne it is a right understanding of death that is a pre-condition of the proper appreciation of life. If death, 'the goal of our career', terrifies us, 'how is it possible to take a single step forward, without fever?' Again and again he insists on the centrality of death to our human experience, and the need to take it into account: 'The premeditation of death is the premeditation of freedom.' He himself has taken the necessary steps: 'I am disengaging myself on all sides: I have more or less taken my leave of everyone, except myself.' To teach men to die, he asserts, is to teach them how to live. To think otherwise is to misunderstand our place in the scheme of things; and it would be absurd to compare our human span with the duration of mountains, rivers, stars, trees. To deny death would be to run away from ourselves: 'C'est une partie de vous que la mort'.

There are various influences at work here, from Lucretius (*De rerum natura*) to scripture ('In the midst of life we are in death'). And as if pre-empting Shakespeare's seven ages of man, Montaigne suggests four ages of the planet – its childhood, then adolescence, virility and old age. But finally, life is not in itself either good or bad: what counts is the good or evil that you impose on it. One of the most attractive aspects of Montaigne's essays is his insistence on keeping the human measure: for him, reason and well-being alike require a just estimate of what is within our grasp, and what is beyond us. And along with this goes a real relish and appetite, a delight in the 'voluptés' that life has to offer.

Flexibility and resilience are fundamental Montaigne virtues. But do they hold to the end? Bronnie Ware, an Australian nurse whose work has included giving palliative care to patients on the verge of death, has compiled a book called *The Top Five Regrets of the Dying* (Hay House, 2012). Heading the list is the failure to be true to oneself, either from personal choice or because it would not have been 'the life others expected of me'. Then, from every male patient and some female patients too (many, being elderly, have come from a generation where women were not breadwinners), the wish not to have worked so hard, with the treadmill of work seen as preventing more time being spent with their children and their partner. The other most frequently stated regrets are not having the courage to express feelings (this is seen as potentially very harmful to health: 'Many developed illnesses relating to the bitterness and resentment they carried'); not keeping in touch with old friends; and not giving oneself permission to be happier ('deep within, they longed to laugh properly and have silliness in their life again.')

It's striking that all these regrets, expressed as wishes, relate so closely to one another and focus so narrowly on the individual concerned. On this evidence, no one seems to regret hurting people or failing to work on behalf of good causes. Maybe this reflects the way the responses were elicited, or the framing of the question; maybe it is just what happens as the machine begins to close down. Either way,

Montaigne took the measure of it all: 'The usefulness of life,' he wrote in the essay on philosophizing and death, 'is not in its span, but the use you make of it.' ('L'utilité du vivre n'est pas en l'espace, elle est en l'usage').

The last essay in the last book of the *Essais* (Book III), 'De l'expérience' has, inevitably, the feeling of a *summa*. And in its final paragraph, Montaigne writes: 'The most beautiful lives are, in my opinion, those that match the common, human model, with order, but without miracle and without extravagance.' ('Les plus belles vies sont, à mon gré, celles qui se rangent au modelle commun et humain, avec ordre, mais sans miracle et sans extravagance.') Montaigne died over four hundred and twenty years ago, on 13 September 1592. For him, the continuing life of the truthful word has easily outflanked death.

UNSTILL LIFE

There are places that manage to outflank their fame and its consequences. Assisi is one, Petra another: and Monet's house and garden at Giverny, north-west of Paris in the department of the Eure, could be a third. Like the other two, it swarms with visitors, many of them somehow able to dissociate their own presence from the crowd, as if distinct from the pullulation rather than adding to it. Perhaps this helpful illusion allows them to see through their fellows and concentrate on the object of their visit – at least, up to a point. I went to Giverny on a bright, clear Sunday morning in early August, arriving in time for the opening of the house and garden at 9.30. Equally punctual were several coachloads of visitors, including one of Japanese tourists and one of elderly Americans. The Japanese, mustard keen and full of chatter, lost no time in deploying their digital cameras. They clicked and clicked, holding their cameras out in front of them like a gestural offering, in an unconscious parody of the Impressionist preoccupation with light and shade. The Americans were a sad crew by comparison, their faces tense with the oncoming and actual ills of decrepitude, their bodies propped on various kinds of metalwork.

By ten o'clock, half an hour after opening time, three queues had established themselves: one of people waiting to view the house; one outside the toilets; and one at the tills in the shop located in what had been Monet's third and largest studio. For sale here, alongside the inevitable reproductions of Monet pictures on tee-shirts, mugs and coasters, greetings cards and the rest, was something more interesting – packets of seeds harvested from plants in the garden: a suggestion of continuity and continuance.

Monet is said to have first caught sight of the village of Giverny in 1883, from the window of a train in which he was travelling – an image which had a pleasing sequel later on in his life, when each morning one of the gardeners would take a boat out onto the lake of the water garden to wipe the water lilies clean of any soot blown across from passing trains.

Giverny, a hillside village of low houses, had at the time a population of some three hundred, mostly farmers. They must have been at the very least curious at the arrival of Monet (whose wife Camille had died in 1879), together with Alice Hoschedé, his two children and her six. Alice was still married to Ernest Hoschedé, a shrewd collector whose artistic judgement was unfortunately far better than his ability to live within his means. He lost no time in disbursing the money accruing to the textiles company he had inherited from his father, and financial ruin was not long in following. But any impression that the village was being invaded by a bohemian artist must soon have been dispelled. Monet's temperament was far more a matter of *flatter le bourgeois* rather than *épater*, as must have been obvious long before he married Alice in 1892, the year following Ernest's death. By then Monet had bought the house and garden and had taken on his first gardener, Félix Bruil.

Today the house, which was restored in the late 1970s, gives every appearance of prosperity. A long building on two floors, it has a wooden veranda right along its south face: from there three short flights of steps, one at either end and one positioned centrally, lead directly down to the garden and the *grande allée*, a gravel walk carpeted with nasturtiums under broad arches covered in due season with climbing roses. All the woodwork, including the house shutters and French windows, are painted a rich green not far off emerald, and the walls are, strikingly, pink roughcast. Up them climb, in profusion, roses and creepers.

Inside, once past the man by the door whose fate it is to intone 'no photos inside' every minute or so, the visitor is free to inspect the fully furnished interior – Monet's studio/sitting room, his bedroom, a spice store – and, perhaps most memorable of all, the dining room (which glows as warmly yellow as any Van Gogh, and where the large table is fully laid with cutlery, plates and glasses) and the kitchen, with its cobalt blue faience tiles from Rouen, and a huge black range. Here and there are small photographs of family groups. Several rooms are hung not only with Monet's own pictures but also with his wonderful collection of Japanese *ukiyo-e* prints by, amongst others, Hokusai, Hiroshige and Utamaro – 'visions of the floating world'. The guidebook suggests that

> with their skilful use of polychrome they captured a world in movement, where all is gesture,...rhythm and cadence. Even the landscapes, both small and large in scale, depicted a life of intensity and motion, the antithesis of stasis.

Yet that word 'stasis' pinpoints a paradox about the house: immaculate as it is following its restoration, the very perfection of it is in danger of emphasising the corollary that is its static nature. Here is the table, with its orderly place settings, at which no meal will again be served, or friends and visitors entertained: there are the made-up beds no occupant will again rumple (and even during Monet's lifetime, the ambience of the house became diminished: no longer quick with friends, children and social occasions, it was reduced to a *ménage* consisting of Monet, his widowed step-daughter Blanche and his surviving son, Michel). However beautiful and genuinely interesting, the restoration inevitably over-simplifies, overlaying with exquisite appearance the human complexities of its gone life. It is a tableau, a moment caught as if in amber.

'En dehors de la peinture et du jardinage, je ne suis bon à rien!', Monet commented in a moment of what may or may not have been real modesty. Either way, for an August visitor, to step down from the house into the garden is to be engulfed in a world of extraordinary exuberance and fecundity ('gardens' rather than 'garden', really, since the walled garden, the Clos Normand immediately to the south of the house, is separated by a road from the plot of land on which Monet created his famous water garden).

Of course it is possible to give an accurate description of the scene in terms of its creation and history, from Monet's protracted attempts to get local authority permission to divert a stream, the Ru, to the virtual re-invention of the garden, some fifty years after Monet's death, thanks largely to the efforts of Gérald van der Kemp who, by the time he came to take an interest in Giverny in the mid-1970s, had already played a leading part in the restoration of Versailles.

Van der Kemp's extraordinary life included arriving in Paris alone at the age of seventeen following his family's ruin in the 1929 crash; joining the Foreign Legion and being posted to Morocco; being taken prisoner in Normandy early on in the second world war, escaping and finding himself in charge of valuable artefacts that the French were anxious to keep out of German hands, including the Mona Lisa and the Venus de Milo. (And like Monet himself, Van der Kemp is buried at Giverny, in the churchyard of Sainte-Radegonde, the church in which Monet was married, and where he regularly attended mass with his family). To return to the Giverny gardens, in practical terms they owe their recreation and continuing existence largely to the work of Gilbert Vahé, head gardener for thirty-five years until 2011, when he was succeeded by an Englishman, James Priest.

It is also perfectly feasible to list the successive plantings together with the names of all the plants; to note, in the Clos Normand, the combination of wild and garden flowers and the presence of many varieties of the same flowers. In bloom at the time of my visit were, amongst scores of others, dahlias (one of Monet's favourites), hollyhocks, nicotianas, cosmos, sunflowers and rudbeckias, while the nasturtiums in the *grande allée* were just beginning to spread their carpet. And there are easily definable contrasts between the colourful vivacity of the Clos Normand and the aqueous greens of the water garden, the feeling of inwardness that has it enclosed in the open secrets of its own reflections. These too can be articulated, along with the Japanese links evident in the water garden with its elegant brow of a bridge (the largest of four), and including even the plaque recording the commemorative plantation donated by the Botanic Park of Toyohashi – azaleas ('fleur municipale de Toyohashi') and jiron kaki ('spécialité de Toyohashi').

Finally, though, it seems almost impossible to convey the overall impact: however comprehensive and colourful, lists of plant names devolve into pallor. Words can barely do justice to the richness of the Clos Normand, with its tall flower-bursts, any more than they can adequately conjure the water garden. Even the domestic note struck by a small chicken run adds to the diversity rather than bringing it within easy reach of lively expression: and the vegetable garden, of which Monet was so proud, is not accessible to visitors.

Perhaps a submerged admission of elusiveness underlies Monet's late series of pictures of the water-garden, the Nymphéas paintings for which he had a huge new studio built, and whose size and fluidity seem an acknowledgement that no frame could contain them. These were the paintings he characterised as 'un tout sans fin, une onde sans horizon et sans rivage' ('an infinite whole, a wave with no horizon and no shore').

There are some experiences, some places even, which artists can hope only to approach rather than to master, whether in words or paint: no doubt part of their fascination lies precisely in their elusiveness. At Giverny the garden riots, the dwelling rests. Seen from the far side of the Clos Normand, the house looks as if it is slowly being engulfed by the upward swarming of the plants: a monument subdued, almost overwhelmed, by the constant renewal of life going on.

The novelist Mary McCarthy, in a 1954 essay published in *Encounter*, 'My Confession', gives a highly persuasive account of the politics of her youth in the early 1930s, capturing exactly the casual, almost feckless way in which causes and attitudes could be taken up or, equally, abandoned. Hearing of Hitler's anti-Jewish atrocities, for instance, 'I had a flurry of political indignation': and when, after graduation, she and her husband first encountered left-wing politics, 'we accepted the need for social reform, but we declined to draw the "logical" inference that the Communists wanted us to draw from this.' Repelled by the humourless zeal of the comrades, she was nonetheless impressed by them, though 'the literary Communists I sincerely despised because I was able to judge the quality of the work they published and see their dishonesty and contradictions.' At one point she finds herself wondering why, having been drawn almost unconsciously into the company and outlook of Communists, she did not actually join the Party:

> Right here, I come up against a puzzle: why didn't I take the next step? But it is only a puzzle if one thinks of me not as a concrete entity but as a term in a logical operation: you agree with the Communist Party; *ergo*, you join it. I reasoned that way but I did not behave so. There was something in me that capriciously resisted being a term in logic, and the very fact that I cannot elicit any specific reason why

> I did not join the Party shows that I was never really contemplating it...

But it took the shenanigans surrounding the indictment and trial of Trotsky to wean McCarthy finally off the Communists, and for her to see that 'Marxism...was something you had to take up young, like ballet dancing.' In fact her essay is as much about being a young student with literary aspirations as it is about political commitment. She evokes very well the sheer excitement and muddle of being young in that context and time – and in doing so reminds us how much depends on chance (as it did for Trotsky) and how individual the contingencies of an evolving life are. It's also interesting to be reminded how, for the young, causes located abroad often have a glamour much more obvious than anything happening at home. Nonetheless I am haunted by a general question underlying the essay – how is it that generation after generation of potential radicals find as they grow older that they have become dilute liberals? And is this necessarily a regressive development?

For all the differences of individual temperament and personal circumstances, it is education that must surely play a crucial part in determining not just what we think, but how we set about thinking. And this will be properly effective only if education can be enabled to fulfil one of its primary tasks, by convincing us that it can be sustained purposefully in adult life and in action. 'Ah, but that is liberal humanism,' someone said to me recently with a shake of the head, 'and that's never been possible for the many'. However true this may be, it hardly adds up to an argument for or against a given educational system. And it's worth considering what happens when education is seen as purely instrumental, designed to make people 'fit for purpose', in that awful phrase, in the context of a capitalist work-driven society (and isn't 'work ethic' in this context virtually an oxymoron?). But what if we look at it the other way round: a capitalist society designed to make people fit for education, and then further education?

It's another American novelist, Marilynne Robinson, who sets out to examine the current state of play, in some of the essays collected in *When I was a child I read books* (Virago, 2012). Lamenting the general loss of a spirit of generosity in public life as in public language, she also deplores the way in which 'our great public education system is being starved and abandoned, and our prisons have declined to levels that disgrace us.' She depicts contemporary society as clamorous and confrontational, a prey to dubious stimulants that militate against reason:

> There are excitements that come with abandoning the constraints of moderation and reasonableness. Those whose work it is to sustain the endless palaver of radio and television increasingly stimulate these excitements...But the effect of this marketing of rancor has unquestionably been to turn debate or controversy increasingly into a form of tribal warfare, harming the national community and risking always greater harm. I think it is reasonable to wonder whether democracy can survive in this atmosphere.

In the same essay she comments drily that 'If we were to retain humane learning and lose a little edge in relative productivity, I would say we had chosen the better part.'

Elsewhere, notably in 'Austerity as Ideology', she writes of the prevailing climate of fear, and 'the current passion for Austerity...as both practical necessity and moral ideal. Anxiety has taken on a life of its own. It has become a sort of succubus on our national life.' For her, 'rationalism and reason are antonyms, the first fixed and incurious, the second open and inductive. Rationalism is forever settling on one model of reality: reason tends toward an appraising interest in things as they come.' The financial perspectives and priorities could be re-jigged: 'Eliminate the overwhelming cost of phantom wars and fools' errands, and humankind might begin to balance its books.'

All this adds up to a powerful challenge, even if it might be objected that Robinson does not sufficiently take global economic ructions into account. Not that she neglects universal perspectives: for her these have everything to do with the unchanging qualities of human nature, not least a capacity for altruism and self-denial, and with the richness available through religious belief. Yet here too she sees the situation as critical:

> ...Christianity does seem to have receded, and dramatically, in just those countries where there are established churches. I say 'does seem' because in my conversations with Europeans I have heard a wistfulness and regret for the loss of Christianity...The established churches have defaulted, and to the extent

> that they are monopolies, their failures have closed off access to Christian life and culture.

In the book's final essay, 'Cosmology', Robinson protects the flank of her argument in favour of religious belief:

> The difference between theism and new atheist science is the difference between mystery and certainty. Certainty is a relic, an atavism, a husk we ought to have outgrown. Mystery is openness to possibility, even at the scale now implied by physics and cosmology. The primordial human tropism toward mystery may well have provided the impetus for all that we have learned.

And she rounds again to the failure of education in both schools and the churches – which she links directly to 'the absence of vigorous and critical study of the humanities.'

Neither McCarthy's alert descriptions of youthful radicalism in 30s America, nor Robinson's faith-driven asseverations can be taken as prescriptive: indeed, both writers are in their different ways firmly against any simplistic nostrum. But they do offer prisms through which to consider the Britain of 2013, with its alarmingly high youth unemployment, its huge and growing inequalities of wealth and opportunity, and a political system pretty much discredited by evidence of corruption and self-interest. It is a time when a label such as 'late capitalism' begins to acquire the sense of an imminent ending to be reached by a slow slide into decadence, without any clear idea of what might follow the decease of the system.

It's more than a quarter of a century since the publication, in the wake of riots, of the Church of England report *Faith in the City*, compiled by an impressive line-up of clergy and academics, with others representing the unions, local government and social workers. (Its full title, often forgotten, was *Faith in the City. A Call to Action by Church and Nation*). The report's wide remit was 'To examine the strengths, insights, problems and needs of the Church's life and mission in Urban Priority Areas and, as a result, to reflect on the challenge which God may be making to Church and Nation: and to make recommendations to appropriate bodies.' These recommendations were to be both to the church and to government (in the event, 38 to the church, and 23 to the government).

The report was to cover clergy staffing levels; training programmes for ordained and lay leaders; liturgical needs; work with children and young people; and the use of buildings. It was also to look at the church's work in industrial mission, social services, social responsibility, church schools and education. In considering the work of the government, it would consider specific issues such as the Rate Support Grant, the Urban Programme, levels of overtime working, Community Programmes, Supplementary Benefit, Child Benefit, the taxation system, ethnic records and housing availability and allocation, homelessness, care in the community, Law Centres and law enforcement.

On its publication the report caused considerable controversy – unsurprisingly, given the clear impossibility of reconciling it with Mrs Thatcher's policies. An unnamed cabinet minister was reported as dismissing it, prior to publication, as 'pure Marxist theology': another Conservative MP claimed the report proved that the Anglican Church was governed by a 'load of Communist clerics'. Margaret Thatcher, herself a Methodist, criticised the report for focusing on action by the state rather than self-help. (This point was subsequently addressed by the Chief Rabbi, Immanuel Jakobovits, in a report of his own arguing for 'a more demanding and more satisfying work ethic' as well as greater individual responsibility and 'trust in and respect for the police' as guarantors of security for minority groups). In 2003 a Commission on Urban Life and Faith was established to review and update the work of *Faith in the City*, with the report *Faithful Cities* being published in May 2006.

These reports have had many good consequences, such as the establishment of the Church Urban Fund, which raised and distributed more than £55 million, and the sequel of a *Faith in the Countryside* report. But it was the original report that had the greatest resonance. Nothing quite like this had happened since Toynbee Hall. Twenty years on, the Dean of Norwich, the Right Reverend Graham Smith, spoke (at a civic service) about its impact:

> At one level it provided the churches of the inner city with a voice, and the voice was to articulate what was being felt and experienced by some of the poorest and most disadvantaged communities in Britain... *Faith in the City* began a movement which was partly political (with a small p), partly theological and partly

> spiritual. In all three senses, it was a beacon of hope to a lot of people: local authorities felt that the dilemmas that they faced with limited resources in the face of overwhelming deprivation were being recognised; the churches on the ground felt that the rest of the Church was waking up to the realities of inner city ministry; and, most important of all, people who were locked into the poverty trap of deprived inner city communities began to feel that perhaps there could be a national understanding of the paralysis which gripped them.

What could be more British than that 'partly political (with a small p)'? And in some lingering subtext lurks the question of disestablishment (a serious issue despite the joke word 'anti-disestablishmentarianism', beloved of precocious children). Wouldn't this, more than at any other time since 1945, have been the moment for the church to declare its autonomy, to become something more than 'the Church of England as by law established'? For the church to liberate itself from the state, with which its conjunction was historically little more than a matter of political convenience and power play, might have been profoundly energizing. It might also have made an upper case of that 'political (with a small p)', not least by engaging the interest and enthusiasm of young people. I have never understood the bias against disestablishment which seems to persist. Those who have argued that the last thing we need is liberation theology along the lines of some South American states are surely out to put the frighteners on people more than anything else:

and it's easy to forget that in Wales the church has been disestablished since 1912, as nicely expressed by 'the church *in* Wales'.

There is much more at stake here than administrative niceties – perhaps even now it is not too late for the church to move in a direction that, if it had been followed earlier, might have achieved much, while also saving Giles Fraser, the Dean of St Paul's, from having to fall on his sword last year after trying, with great integrity, to square the cogent principles represented by the Occupy protesters with the demands of the establishment. And it might even, in our age of outsourcing and undemocratically appointed agencies, give a good name to the notion of contracting out. Most of all, disestablishment might strengthen the clarity of the church's message, as well as profoundly affecting our sense of civic society and politics. It may be that disestablishment will come about only when issues such as gay marriage open up a gap between church and state.

I write as one of a generation, and a background, generously favoured by fortune. And I owe a great deal to the country that gave a home to my father when he left Germany in 1934: though he was technically entitled to a British passport, there was also an underwriting generosity at work here. When it comes to good fortune, it's said that 1947 is the ideal year in which to have been born, from the point of view of such advantages as free education, a society becoming increasingly mobile and liberal, employment opportunities – and, after that, a decent pension falling due at a reasonable age. Born five years earlier, I feel much the same, but lament all the more the cramping limitations and deficiencies of the present social and political climate. Not that a bleeding heart is of any use: and if only action is what counts, then I am aware how little I have succeeded in articulating my beliefs in any real political activism. Nor have I come to terms with the conundrum of self-avowedly free democracies such as America and the United Kingdom harbouring the grotesque anomalies as Guantanamo Bay and Yarl's Wood, along with all too many other instances of secrecy and justice delayed or denied.

So, now, I feel that I am offering nothing more than the bobbing witness of a message in a bottle. The nagging question persists – was there a moment, amid the exuberant muddle of youth, whose political import I failed properly to grasp and act on? The Bay of Pigs? Kennedy's assassination? Most likely it was neither of these, but rather Vietnam, where it became obvious, as we see now once more only too clearly in Iraq and Afghanistan, that political problems (even those involving oil) very rarely have military solutions. And it was precisely the prospect of war in Iraq that produced a startling display of political commitment and impotence together. 'Not in my name', declared a million and a half vehement protesters: and the government promptly went to war, justifying its decision by evidence that has come to look increasingly dubious. It's clear that the emergence of the internet, facebook, tweeting and the like have made possible the swift exchange of information, including the planning of action, in an entirely new way. It remains to be seen whether in time this will somehow facilitate the emergence of a new political forum that combines civic responsibility with real clout: and that understands education as an end, not just a means.

FLIGHTS

for John Moat

Images for the workings of the imagination are plentiful, from Shakespeare's airy nothings finding a local habitation, to Nabokov's comment that 'Our imagination flies – we are its shadow on the earth'. This association with the airborne, in one way or another, is perhaps the most common way of characterising the imagination – as a bird taking wing, in flights of fancy, alighting here and there as it pleases, or tempted down.

There are, of course, no formulæ; nor is it possible to list the conditions in which the imagination will necessarily flourish. On the other hand, it is perfectly possible to describe personal or social conditions inimical to its thriving: acute pain; a society predicated on busyness; an education system with no built-in pauses; oppression; clamour. In this sense the readiest definitions are negative. But at what point, and how, might these be transformed – so that the howl of pain may become a song of lamentation, or an understanding of the impact of seething activity and noise heighten a creative awareness of their opposites?

•

In truth the imagination is not anarchic but, rather, anachronistic: not against order (though its imperatives are likely to diverge fundamentally from those of politicians and artocrats), but against time. The confinement it really challenges is that of mortality.

•

The ultimate negativity: can you imagine a world without the imagination?

•

Precisely what makes the imagination so exhilarating is its inherent combination of paradigm and instance, potential and enactment. What other entity combines these qualities of unchanging substance and limitless variation, of innocence and usage, the universal and the individual?

•

Another joy of the imagination is the way in which it brings together discovery and recognition.

•

If a hologram is cut or broken into any number of pieces, each fragment – while still individual in its own shape – retains an image of the whole, even if in lower resolution. This strikes me as an apt emblem for the relation between the imagination and its individual manifestations.

•

In the 1950s there was a hot-rod American evangelical preacher (operating, I think, under the name Colonel Samson, a kind of *nom de doom*) who toured a number of British schools. One of the two sermons he offered began, unforgettably: 'If I had a million dollars, I would build a mighty monument a hundred miles long and a hundred miles wide and a hundred miles high, and I would call it "the mighty failure"'. More recently we have had the Millennium Dome, a fine instance of putting the cart before the horse. In the realm of the imagination, there can be similar temptations – not least the desire to have a Career as a Writer or Poet, all upper case.

•

There are times when the imagination promotes a creative ability to keep the eye off the ball. For the poet, sometimes, this can take the form of the shadow poem that emerges, paradoxically, as a bonus of intense concentration on another poem: the poem in hand joined by at least one from the bush.

•

Insofar as the imagination has to do with community and communication, you'd think the present time would be an advantageous one. It's an irony that the age of broadband can be so narrowing, and to find that globalisation has fragmentation as its corollary. It's hard to talk of this without appearing luddite, and of course new generations will find their own idioms and emphases and know, more than their elders might give them credit for, what weight and worth to give to new technologies. These may be indeed simply beyond the imaginative reach of those brought up with carbon paper and the use of a razor blade to correct typing errors. Yet, whatever adaptive virtues and skills may emerge, it's also hard not be concerned about the consequences, actual and potential, of our new systems. Some of these centre on the simple matter of speed: the risks of approximation, superficiality, a lack of giving proper consideration.

•

One definition of good teaching in schools: smuggling the imagination through.

•

The imagination delights in mirrors and games, and can accommodate easily what we only imagine we imagine.

•

At the frontiers of utilitarian relevance, perhaps the imagination has nothing to declare. Yet hasn't it often been a leap of the imagination that has enabled the crossing of the threshold to discoveries, some with important practical implications?

•

Paying attention, a form of slowing down, is often a threshold to the imagination, as can be also, for children, the experience of boredom. For adults, on a car journey it's good to be able to view a breakdown as an invitation to study the verges usually raced past in a blur.

•

Sometimes the workings of the imagination are curtailed by being committed too soon to paper or screen. As a culture we have recourse to the written word very readily: it's interesting to see what may happen when, instead of reaching for the notebook as soon as an image or an idea occurs, we harbour and hatch.

•

Those who disbelieve the environmental consequences of human exploitation and pollution may be suffering not only from denial, but a failure of the imagination, whose logic would tell them that one possible outcome of a consumer society is a cannibal society.

•

I once invited a student to tell me the tense of a verb in a French text we were reading. He thought for some time, in the way people do when they haven't a clue but feel they should give an impression of deep contemplation and effort, goodwill standing in for knowledge. Finally he ventured, 'Is it the operatic present?' Perhaps the proper tense for the workings of the imagination would be 'the infinite present'. And here is the unwritten page.

•

Flights – fancy, yes; escape, yes; but without them the arrow could not hit its target.

ALCESTE AND THE QUIET COACH

Even in their privatised state, so to speak, the railways offer (and for no extra charge) outstanding opportunities to study the more gladiatorial aspects of human behaviour. The chagrin of different parties holding identical seat reservations, the discovery that someone else is in your reserved seat and very reluctant to move, the struggle to hoist luggage onto the undersized overhead rack, the person with a large rucksack who slugs you in passing – all these have their part to play. In addition, there is always the possibility of a lost ticket, or the wrong type of ticket, either of which is likely to mean buying another one at maximum cost. For older passengers, even supposing they have remembered their railcard, thus avoiding a supplementary charge, there are still the singular variants of English to fulminate pleasurably against: you can see the glint in their eyes as the 'train manager' announces himself, followed by the girl running the buffet doing likewise: she is the 'customer host'. This can be followed by the wonder of an Irish version of H, as in 'Coach Haytch' (isn't usage meant to take the easiest route, when it comes to pronunciation? Know-a-mean?) or the imparting, just short of Reading, of the quasi-pugilistic news that 'we are waiting to be platformed'. Trains are always waiting to be platformed at Reading.

None of these stimulants, however, has quite the power of the quiet coach as a breeding-ground for fury. Simply by being defined as a space where you are asked not to use your mobile phone or personal stereo, and to keep conversation to the secular equivalent of a reverential hush, the quiet coach is able to attract such devotees as a party of eight or so heading to the coast, wearing sombreros and identical tee-shirts, and passing round more than several bottles of *prosecco*; a man loudly briefing a work colleague on the details of a legal dispute or the likely state of the stock market next week; a person jerkily possessed by the music that his headphones are unable to contain and whose eye it seems best not to catch; a woman on her mobile intent on bellowing to a friend the hilarious details of the holiday in the sun from which she has just returned; or an elderly person who, taking the supposed benefits of the quiet carriage too literally, has descended into a rattling snore. Compared with any of this, the man who only once during the journey emits the kind of sneeze which would endanger the fabric of the Albert Hall is as nothing.

The other two standard features of the quiet carriage are, in no particular order, the passenger (sorry, 'customer') who clearly would like to quell the source or sources of noise, but is temperamentally unsuited to doing so (he or she spends much time swivelling in search of someone who might undertake the task, attempting to encourage such a person by a look of pitiful distress designed to appeal to gallantry) – and the person who indeed intervenes on behalf of the promised tranquillity.

Such intervention can be made in a number of ways: at one end of the scale, as a low-key request, tempered by a smile that seems to acknowledge almost apologetically the relatively footling nature of the matter – or, at the other, in a state not far removed from quivering apoplexy fuelled by the kind of righteous indignation that keeps cardiologists in demand.

Most commonly, what ensues is a terrible awkwardness or anger on both sides: you can tell that both parties feel they have been uncomfortably, even outrageously, exposed in some way. The noise-maker fumes, blusters, either turns off the noise source with bad grace or even imports the whole incident into the mobile phone conversation: 'I'm in the quiet carriage, *apparently*' (oh yeah?), 'and this fascist prat has asked me to stop, so I'll try again from Taunton'. Or the accused may choose to persist, daring the ambassador of silence to try again. Or else the accuser, having succeeded, returns to his seat not realising how lucky he is not to have been platformed, and with a look of satisfaction that is meant to be modest but which half expects (and sometimes even gets) the congratulations of other passengers: the smug solidarity of those who know they are in the right. The atmosphere of the quiet carriage has now achieved all the prickly unease of an armed truce.

Anger is something to be avoided, according to Bacon in his essay 'Of regiment of health', as something 'fretting inwards'. He obviously understood its potential for corroding the soul. More often, though, anger is a social vice – and not always seen as a vice, at that. Cardinal Manning, for one, saw it as 'the executive power of justice', though had he lived long enough he would probably have been startled by the application of this view to Sidney Lumet's memorable film (based on a television play by Reginald Rose) *Twelve Angry Men*. In this tense story, an Hispanic teenager faces the electric chair if found guilty of murdering his father: the decision rests with the jurors. It seems a straightforward case, but one of the jurors (played by Henry Fonda) thinks – to the irritation of his fellow jurors – that it would be correct to review the evidence, however briefly (a good instance, this, of dramatic exposition fitting exactly with the plot). The story of how the pendulum swings, with one after another juror changing his mind, is well known. At key points it is anger that enables the unlocking of the personal truth underlying a juror's decision – one is a racist; another has fallen out with his own teenage son (he is the last to change his mind). The oldest juror is alone in spotting a possible reason for the flawed evidence of an elderly witness to the crime, while another, raised in a rough neighbourhood, has witnessed enough knife fights to know that the defendant probably couldn't have inflicted the victim's wound. Nonetheless, it is impossible to think that the final verdict of innocence could have come about without the spur of anger.

For the real connoisseur of anger, it would be hard to better Alceste, the central character of Molière's 1666 play *Le Misanthrope*. Alceste has a problem, and one of which he is proud, namely the compulsion to say exactly what he thinks in any given situation. At the same time, he is outraged by the hypocrisy and duplicity of his fellow humans: indeed, anger is his default mode. In our own time he would long, you feel, to achieve the righteous end of being mown down on a zebra crossing.

It doesn't help that he is in love with Célimène, a young widow of twenty already well versed in the ways of the world, and with a considerable capacity for flightiness and gossip. Alceste's feelings for Célimène are his Achilles heel, a joke on the part of the gods – curmudgeon meets flirt; and the subtitle of the play, *L'Amant Atrabilaire* (*The Bilious Lover*), is a reminder that emotions apparently universal in their scope may be symptoms with very particular causes. In any case, the kind of reassurance Alceste seeks from Célimène about her feelings for him is simply not available on the terms, or in the terms, he wants: he cannot settle for her reassurance, genuine as it seems, that he has 'le bonheur de savoir que vous êtes aimé' ('the good fortune of knowing that you are loved').

So far, so straightforward – but what makes this, for me, one of Molière's greatest plays, is the ambivalence of the comedy. On one level Alceste ('l'homme aux rubans verts' – green, the colour of envy and so of anger) is plainly ridiculous; on another, for all his raging he has a point. The play is a high-wire act, balancing between Alceste's brutal frankness and the insincerity that social conduct ineluctably involves. Though it never abandons the comic mode, this is also a play about the unknowability of others, the inconsistency of human nature and the need (which can be consuming) to know the truth, especially in matters of the heart. Re-reading it, I think it is about the essential nature of trust almost as much as the comic juxtaposition of extremism and *honnêteté*, a contest greatly enriched by being couched in alexandrines, with rolling tides of *précieux* agglomeration and ellipses heightened by rhyme.

The play shows anger as, like the tango, a game for at least two players: exercised in solitude it remains essentially pathological rather than dramatic. Alceste's intention of heading for a desert to live apart from society is as comic as his feelings for Célimène, whose whole well-being is predicated upon the enjoyable vicissitudes of a narrow society with clearly defined boundaries of etiquette and acceptability. Equally unrealistic is his intemperate demand that she should follow him into the wilderness – precisely because what Alceste and Célimène have profoundly in common is the need for an audience. 'L'ami du genre humain n'est point du tout mon fait' ('the friend of the human race is certainly not for me') protests Alceste in the play's opening scene – but where would he be without others?

I wonder whether the luke-warmth of the play's initial reception wasn't in some measure due to its nearness to the bone. For all the comic exaggeration – Oronte with his absurd sonnet demanding to have Alceste's honest opinion (and scandalised when he gets it, even if it takes Alceste some time to deploy his declared preference for total honesty); Acaste and Clitandre, fops enveloped in a talcum cloud of rhetoric and hot air; Alceste himself with his propensity for declaring the entire human race detestable; Célimène bitching wittily about those around her – there is, nevertheless, some discomfiture in the admission that Alceste's protestations cannot be dismissed entirely. 'Et la sincérité dont son âme se pique / A quelque chose, en soi, de noble et d'héroïque', ('And his candour, his soul's nervous tic / Has something inherently noble and heroic') as Éliante observes in act IV, scene I – and this despite the fact that Alceste, furious with Célimène, has insultingly offered Éliante his affection as a *pis aller*. For all his fulminations, Alceste somehow retains the affection of those around him to an extent that suggests there is something more than just endearing about him, absurd and impractical as his clamouring for total candour may be. And the curlicues of language lead to the deployment of some pretty heavy weaponry, as in the confrontation between Célimène and the prudish and judgemental Arsinoé, whose apparent devotion to virtue cannot conceal her own agenda, which includes the hope that Alceste will redirect his attentions to her.

It could be said that the whole dynamic of the action relies on anger and the energies it generates, from Alceste's opening tirades against insincerity ('Ce commerce honteux de semblants d'amitié' – 'This shameful commerce of false friendship') to his professed intention at the end of the play to go off into the wilderness, where he envisages a life untainted by contact with humans. The action is propelled by a series of confrontations: Alceste and Oronte, Célimène and Arsinoé, Alceste and Célimène. The ensuing dissonances are calmly conducted from centre field by the measure of Philinte's and Eliante's sweet reasonableness: the world is as it is, and will not be changed by any number of censorious judgements. Yet, imperfect as society is in many respects, 'La parfaite raison fuit toute extrémité' ('Perfect reason recoils from all extremes') as Philinte observes in the opening scene.

Alceste's anger exposes his real character. What he thinks of as love is, in truth, a frightened need for reassurance, expressed as possessiveness: and his indignation, his constant demands for justice, are symptomatic of a chronic lack of confidence. You could say that Alceste is not so much sincere as involuntarily transparent, and actually predictable. Psychologically, it would be understandable that at some level Alceste is himself aware of this, and that this would serve only to intensify his rage. Much as, in the quiet carriage, the complainant against noise might feel that, even with right on his or her side, there is the unpleasant sensation of being over-exposed. None of which stifles the audience's laughter.

Postscript

Since writing this essay, I have experienced an instance not of quiet coach anger, but something quite other. The man next to me on the London train, thirty-something I would guess and encased in headphones, had been attending – perfectly quietly, indeed – to his laptop. Shortly after finishing his work and closing the machine, he suddenly lunged forward and plucked a sealed plastic triangle from his bag. He turned to me, waving it in the air. 'Do you mind?' he asked; and then, seeing my startled look, explained, 'It's a sandwich. Do you mind if I eat it?' I was almost lost for words in the face of such elegant consideration, but did express surprise that he felt the need to ask. 'Well,' he said, 'it is the quiet carriage, and some people wouldn't like the smell.' Ah.

GOD'S IDEOGRAMS

In the churchyard of a village by the Thames, in early 2001, my twin sister and I stood by the priest who held the plastic container, not much smaller than a sweet jar, with my mother's ashes. He said a prayer or two, unscrewed the lid and poured. With a slight shifting sound, the dark coarse talcum fell onto the prepared earth, beside the upturned lid of turf which would cover the ashes. It sent up a thin veil of dust that dispersed quickly.

How we long for certainty! For the features imprinted on the Turin shroud really to be the features of Christ; for the retail opportunity exploited so successfully by the emperor Constantine's mother Helena to have involved pieces of wood that really were fragments of the True Cross; for the resurrection of the body. Philip Larkin, at the end of his poem 'An Arundel Tomb', wrote memorably of the human urge 'to prove / Our almost-instinct almost true: / What will survive of us is love'. And of course that actually is true (for all Larkin's wary mid-course corrections enacted by the repeated 'almost'), even though it holds out no greater prospect than a residue that will, sooner or later, inexorably dwindle. But it is also more credible than Stanley Spencer's painting of the general resurrection, with its hale figures clambering out of their graves a little further downstream at Cookham, where they had been parked.

In Exeter, the small city where I live, you see them streaming out on Sundays – the Roman Catholics and the Baptists from their adjacent churches in South Street; the

Anglicans across the cathedral green, and from the city's parish churches; the Methodists from the Mint in Fore Street; the Presbyterians and Congregationalists from the United Reformed church in Southernhay; the Evangelicals from Belmont Chapel on the inner by-pass; the Jehovah's Witnesses from Kingdom Hall on the Topsham Road; the Quakers from the meeting house behind Wynards; and on Fridays after prayers, the Muslims from the mosque in York Road. Elsewhere and in their own times and places come Mormons, Hindus, Christian Scientists, Sikhs, Buddhists, Seventh-day Adventists, the Greek and Russian Orthodox believers, Plymouth Brethren – and, no doubt, others I have failed to name.

Can they all be right? Can they all be wrong? 'Man is out of his mind,' wrote Montaigne. 'He would not know how to fashion a maggot, and fashions gods by the dozen.' ('L'homme est bien insensé. Il ne saurait forger un ciron, et forge des Dieux à douzaines.') But perhaps the sacred, as much as the poetic, requires 'a local habitation and a name', with the plurality this would involve.

For those who find the whole thing too much, there is always the possibility of Pascal's famous wager – that it is better to believe in God since, if he exists, that will prove to have been prudent; and if he doesn't, nothing will have been lost. But this particular sophistry could well be an underestimate of God's capacity (if he exists) for comprehending the human capacity for wriggling.

The recently retired Archbishop of Canterbury has said that you cannot cherry-pick the components of your belief, and of course from his viewpoint that is absolutely right. But don't fallible mortals inevitably cherry-pick? Are there not, particularly in the detail of a given church's emphases and rituals, some aspects of belief and worship to which many people assent less easily than to others? Even though it's alarmingly possible for the real energizing nature of faith to go missing somewhere in the gaps between literalism and metaphor, how many churchgoers would accept the bible in its entirety? There are, probably, nearly as many answers to this question as there are denominations and sects: and the answer you give is likely to depend on personal temperament as well as experience.

For me, a real obstacle is the church's proclaimed aim of proselytizing. It is one thing to hold to faith, but quite another to impose it on others. And historically the desire to bring redemption to those in ignorance has led to appalling violence on every level: here is certainty in its murderous mode. In this context, it's hard to ignore the chill example of Victorian missionary work, as characterised by Lewis Hensley's hymn – 'O'er heathen lands afar, / thick darkness broodeth yet'; likewise the irony of the slow-flying boomerang effect it has produced. Now, it is precisely dogged adherence to traditional biblical beliefs on the part of the countries to which the missionaries went out that threatens a radical split in the Anglican Communion. No sex outside marriage for them, let alone gay partnerships of any kind.

But even if you leave the matter of proselytizing aside, what about the evidence presented by the world as it is? Voltaire, in *Candide*, finds himself unable to circumvent the ambiguities of the world in its manicheistic opposition of good and evil, a struggle in which virtue is frequently punished and vice rewarded, while the church is all too often on the wrong side. Cue our contemporary horror stories of child abuse perpetrated by those clad in God's livery. And then there is the question of natural disasters, stumbling-blocks such as the Lisbon earthquake of 1755, which provoked Voltaire to write a long poem (*Poème sur le désastre de Lisbonne*) and which also features in *Candide*. Either God was powerless to prevent such things, in which case he would be transgressing the Trades Descriptions Act, or he allowed such things to happen and was therefore a cruel god. And, pointedly, those who are virtuous in *Candide* are either non-believers or, like James the Anabaptist (who loses his life trying to save a villainous sailor from drowning), beyond the embrace of the mainstream church.

In matters of belief, so much must depend on personal experience. How do you come to faith? It can be adventitious indeed, and it doesn't have to be in the family – witness the story of a friend, Sally Read, a fellow writer who lives in Italy and who, coming from a background of firm atheism, began at the age of forty to find her own remarkable way towards belief. In her account, one of the most striking moments concerns a time when prayer was something she could not do:

> I didn't know how to pray; I had never prayed. Nonetheless, each day I stopped off at a little Carmelite church by the sea to sit and listen. I was open to the presence of God, but I was still not Christian – and far from Catholic. In that church, there was an icon of Christ and, prayerless, I would simply look at him.

> It was on one of these occasions that I spoke aloud to the face and asked for help. There was no visual or aural hallucination, or anything, as a poet, I can use as a metaphor to tell what happened. The nearest I can come to describing it is to say that it felt like I was an amnesiac in a fit of quiet panic, and suddenly someone walked into the room that I recognised. Later, I would read Simone Weil's account of a very similar experience: 'Christ lui-même est descendu et m'a prise.'

She captures very well the intensity of her growing faith, in an idiom that recalls the experience of others who have not so much come to God as failed to escape him: 'I came to realise that the smell, the taste, the touch, the sound of God outfoxed the mind. I could rationalise, but all my rationalising couldn't alter the profound rationality of my encounter with God.' Finally she was received into the Roman Catholic church, an institution that she describes rapturously, and interestingly, as 'an intricate composition of allegory and reality, that tries to give image to God's presence on earth.'

Those who, unlike my friend, find themselves in a state of doubt rather than grace cannot, like Thomas, have the reassurance of palping Christ's wounds, though they might take some comfort from Hector's words in *Troilus and Cressida* (act II, scene 2): 'Modest doubt is call'd / The beacon of the wise.' And, though it is a commonplace that quotations from the bible can be used to prove almost anything, here too there is consolation to be had, in the possibility of God's spacious view of what matters:

> Not every one that saith unto me, Lord, Lord, shall enter into the kingdom of heaven; but he that doeth the will of my father who is in heaven. *Matthew 7.21*

> By their fruits shall ye know them. *Matthew 7.16*

> In my father's house are many mansions. *John 14.2*

Insofar as belief is a matter of an individual decision (and there would be differing opinions about that, too), much may depend on your basic view of the human creature. Does human nature require the discipline of allegiance to a religion, not just faith in the idea of a god? In other words, is it in any sense 'fallen' ? (Or is this an irrelevant question in the perspective of God's capacity for understanding?) Or can human beings sustain, by themselves, the desirable consequences of belief? Is your view of human nature that man is inherently aberrant, despite his best intentions ('Es irrt der Mensch, so lang er strebt', as Goethe has it in *Faust*: 'Man errs as long as he strives'), or do you subscribe to the more confident humanist view? Do you think of community as solely referring to those who share a neighbourhood or a culture, or do you see it embracing all those, world-wide, who are on the side of good – what Christians might call, in a rather clumsy locution, 'the communion of saints'?

In some faiths, the name of God is not even to be spoken, just as Muslims reject any divine iconography. Yet the figure of Christ on the cross, whatever else it may be, is a potent image for the cruelty and suffering that humans inflict on one another every day. Think of those Spanish or Colombian representations that verge on making pain look glamorous, and Grünwald's 'Crucifixion' almost anodyne by comparison.

Candide ends in a garden which, though far removed from Eden, is still a place where vegetables may be grown, and where Cunégonde, no longer beautiful after all that she has suffered, puts delicious pastries on the table. But the price is high, and the god of salvage won't quite do. In many ways the best cards in Voltaire's philosophical tale are given to the atheist Martin: and when at the end of the story he advises 'travaillons sans raisonner: c'est le seul moyen de rendre la vie supportable' ('let us work without reasoning: it is the only way to make life bearable'), the reader must decide whether to think of 'raisonner' as an admission of the futility of debate, or of the mystery of the human condition. 'Mystery' – the word derives partly from the root of a Greek word meaning 'to close the lips or eyes'. I like the meditative, quietist sense of that.

There is no doubting the loss of Christian reference in our culture: nowadays a secondary school class is likely to be as baffled by a quotation from the psalms as they are by their teacher's professed ignorance of a given TV soap. Yet I find it impossible to think of bringing up children without a notion of God, even if the very word 'notion' will seem callow to many believers. As in so much else, there will be time enough later for them to reach their own conclusions: as a parent, I want them to know simply that there are choices. And, to put it in the terms of Pascal's wager, we should be readier to consider what we gain from faith, rather than what we stand not to lose: I find it impossible to conceive of a joyless God.

When it comes to the churches, considered at their best it's hard to think of any other institutions that hold open the door to generosity and compassion on a greater scale or with a broader reach. And when it comes to an idea of God, nothing else quite occupies that space: if the street seems overcrowded, even with its many mansions, we could perhaps learn to think of all forms of religious belief as in some sense ideograms of God, while observing the modes and manners of our local habitation. And isn't the impulse to pray close to being a universal?

I do not subscribe to the view of those who consider dependency always to be a defect rather than a potential strength. I still want to pray in these words, to me potent despite their old usage and their specificity: 'Lord, I believe: help thou my unbelief'. The poet R. S. Thomas, so much of whose work wrestles with a *deus absconditus*, captures this essential presence/absence of God powerfully in 'The Absence', which ends:

> My equations fail
> as my words do. What resource have I
> other than the emptiness without him of my whole
> being, a vacuum he may not abhor?

KAFKA'S SINGING MOUSE

Thanks to a friend who is a music agent, I sometimes go with him to the Green Room at the end of a concert, to see the performers. The atmosphere exudes elation and exhaustion together, along with the still active components of an adrenalin high. On one such occasion I caught sight of a woman singer slumped on a wall seat, her eyes closed. She looked worn out and may have been asleep. I was struck by the air of defencelessness that attached to her, a consequence perhaps of her sleeping; but also by an aura of serenity and strength. She was, essentially, an instrument: I imagined that someone might appear to fold her away into the black velvet lining of a tailored case.

Perhaps more than any other performer, the singer risks exposure of the soul. Without the intermediary – or the protective cover – of a separate music-making device, there has also to be a complete reliance on the expressive capacity and skill contained in the body: no other instrument has quite this physiological dependency.

There is, of course, a long history of the closeness of vulnerability to strength, as in the story of Philoctetes with his malodorous wound resulting from a snake-bite: healed finally by the physician Asclepius, he played a major role in the capture of Troy, killing Paris in single combat. Edmund Wilson, writing in *The Wound and the Bow* (W.H. Allen, 1941; revised edition, 1952), notes 'the conception of superior strength as inseparable from disability' and suggests that in Gide's version (*Philoctète*) 'we come close to a further implication... the idea that genius and disease, like strength and mutilation, may be inextricably bound up together'. The Romantics, not to mention the *poètes maudits*, exemplify the narrowness of the strait between blessing and curse, and in thinking of the frailty that can accompany an artistic sensibility we have only to conjure the image of the consumptive. In English literature, one of the clearest metaphorical articulations of this correspondence comes in one of Eliot's *Four Quartets*, 'East Coker':

> The wounded surgeon plies the steel
> That questions the distempered part;
> Beneath the bleeding hands we feel
> The sharp compassion of the healer's art
> Resolving the enigma of the fever chart.

Here is suffering in its sacerdotal element, where not just vulnerability but actual hurt is seen almost as a pre-condition of healing. Here no redemption or 'sharp compassion' is possible without the understanding induced by the actual experience of being wounded. And the healing has to be personal before it can benefit others:

> If to be warmed, then I must freeze
> And quake in frigid purgatorial fires
> Of which the flame is roses, and the smoke is briars.

There is clearly a specifically Christian dimension at work here, not just in the symbolism of the rose or the echoes in 'briars' and in 'sharp compassion', where 'sharp' could apply as well to the crown of thorns as to the surgeon's scalpel, but in the implication that Christ's passion is the ground of compassion.

In the world of the artist, there would seem to be dangerously little distinction between the blessed and the cursed, the gifted and the afflicted. There is also the ambiguity of suffering in itself, where it is not only a testing human experience but an apparent authentication of the art that ensues, as if endowing it with a value not available in other ways. Such is certainly the case for Josefine, the singing mouse which is the protagonist of Kafka's last story. Narrated by one of the 'mouse people', the story is a wonderfully witty and shrewd examination of the ambiguous relations between artist and audience. Both sides of the equation are present from the outset, as given in the alternative title – *Josefine, die Sängerin, oder das Volk der Mäuse*. The narrator is the spokesrodent for the whole tribe, and the reader is left in no doubt that Josefine operates by courtesy of the general will. She is 'our singer', and the predominant perspective is that of 'our species as a whole'. We learn that, as a matter of fact, the collective preference of the mice, used as they are to hardship and danger, and endowed with 'a certain practical slyness', is for silence. There is a sense in which Josefine is allowed to perform on sufferance, as a kind of exception: when she goes, the narrator observes, 'music will vanish from our lives'. Yet it's not altogether clear whether her utterance is 'Gesang' or only 'Pfeifen', squeaking – to appreciate her art you have to see as well as hear her. Josefine herself denies that there is any similarity between her singing and mere 'Pfeifen'. Here and elsewhere Kafka cunningly develops and maintains the ambiguity of Josefine's situation. Do the mice need her or not? Is she an adornment, a necessity or a nuisance? And is the evaluation of art a matter of aesthetics, technique or societal structure?

Josefine wants not only to be admired, but to be admired on her own terms: and so she is, it seems. When she sings, the audience falls silent. But is this due to her singing, or to 'the solemn silence, by which the weak small voice is surrounded'? In any case the audience, though delighted, has only limited understanding, in Josefine's opinion – 'but she has long since learnt to do without real comprehension.'

The relationship of artist and audience remains complex in Kafka's story. Times are difficult, burdensome. For Josefine, 'it is as if she had put all her strength into her song', and she feels vulnerable, 'laid bare, at the mercy'. The crowd, despite some detractors and sceptics, remains warmly appreciative, bathed in a collective cosiness. Usually Josefine has only to take up a stance indicating her intention to sing for a crowd to gather. But if circumstances hinder the quick arrival of hearers, she rages – swears, even bites. Efforts are made to assemble an audience without her knowing: she is indulged.

'What impels the people to take such trouble for Josefine?' asks the narrator, going on to point out that their devotion to her is not unconditional. They would never laugh at her, though she is in some respects risible. Sometimes it is as if the people feels protective towards her in her neediness, though why remains unclear. But Josefine thinks *she* is protecting *them*. This is illusory – 'das Volk', amid all its tribulations, has learnt to fend for itself. And yet 'it is true, that precisely in situations of need we listen more attentively than otherwise to Josefine's voice.'

Gradually the emphasis shifts. The concerts are sometimes more like an assembly of the people, whose feelings Josefine's singing is there to articulate (but, the narrator adds, a truly first-class singer would not be tolerated). The readiness to heed Josefine is seen as partly due to the short lifespan of the mice combined with their fertility, which together conspire to heap one generation on another, allowing little time for childhood. Thus something childlike lives on into adulthood, a feature from which Josefine has always benefited.

Things don't get any better: when the mice are in danger or under attack Josefine is always the first to make good her escape (and perhaps it is her squeaking that has attracted the attackers). And then, from the outset, she has always demanded freedom from work: singing is effortful enough. What she really craves is 'acknowledgement.'

Finally the matter becomes confrontational. Josefine will, if necessary, use unscrupulous means to attain her ends: rumour has it that she is threatening to shorten her coloraturas. She alleges a foot injury which will mean curtailing her performances, as she has to stand to sing. No one believes her. Other excuses follow. She collapses, seems to rally in a final performance, then vanishes: 'This time she has left us for good.'

In this conflict, it is Josefine who suffers. The 'Volk' trundles on. She is 'a small episode in the eternal history of our people': for her, there remains only the apotheosis of historical anonymity. She will 'happily be assimilated into the countless multitude of our people's heroes'.

The terms and conditions of the compact between artist and audience are constantly changed or modified in this story, so skilfully that the reader may wonder whether either side comes out of it well. But along the way Kafka, for all the lightness of tone, raises some weighty issues. Is the artist a litmus paper for the state of society? Or a lightning conductor? A shaman or a sham? A scapegoat? Any or all of these things, or not quite? The question remains relevant to our own time, not least given the contemporary evidence of artists exploiting the surmounting of artistic judgements by the market and, in an age of nervous investors, the conflation of price and any more artistically based sense of value. If you are lucky, what you collect are your winnings.

Of the three other stories in Kafka's final collection, two – 'First Sorrow', (with its brilliant image of a trapeze artist in the netting luggage rack of a train compartment) and 'The Hunger Artist' – are also to do with performers of a kind. Both focus on the isolation and dependency of the artist; both include an agent/impresario figure, on whose actions and decisions the welfare of the artist depends. And both picture the art in question as involuntary, pathological almost: the protagonists are like suffering Christ-figures, but without a cause. The trapeze artist can exist only in an airborne eyrie; the hunger artist would have eaten if he could have. For him, the single certainty is that the body enacts a swansong. The reader is left with the idea that for the artist work is an ineluctable imperative that may or may not chime with circumstance. And in this lies severe, perhaps fatal confinement, as well as freedom of a kind.

NOTHING TO DECLARE

Heaven knows how many thousands of stories are housed on Ellis Island, in America's Immigration Museum. Represented by photographs, chattels, personal belongings, they are the recorded experiences of the twelve million or so immigrants who passed through there when it was active as an immigration station. As a first-time visitor, I found one of the most haunting stories the account of a Russian family arriving with several large suitcases which had, of course, to be opened for inspection in the Baggage Room. To the astonishment of the presiding official, the cases turned out to contain nothing at all. Asked why they had schlepped this useless luggage all the way across Europe and the Atlantic, the father of the family explained that when it came to leaving home, they did not want their neighbours, or those they might meet on the way, to see how few possessions they had: better the air-filled cases than evidence of penury.

You might think this is a perfect parable about bourgeois pride and impressing the Joneskis – but what has kept it in my mind is what it might be held to convey about the human imagination, seen as that dark emptiness, a figure for the immaterial outflanking the actual and so preserving its potential, its integrity. Think of it, if you like, as a three-dimensional representation of Keats's Negative Capability, with its state of 'being in uncertainties, mysteries, doubts'; or the idea of the writer – and for that matter the reader, being 'the guests of zero', in a striking phrase from a poem by Philip Gross.

Such conjuring of the ethereal may seem out of kilter, if not downright incompatible, with the feverish flow of prescriptive definitions and declarations which poetry has always called forth, and which would seem to demand that every case slapped down on the customs house counter is a revelation.

A thought-provoking conspectus of what poetry might be is to be found in *The Bloodaxe Book of Poetry Quotations* (Bloodaxe Books, 2006). Edited by the Irish poet and critic Dennis O'Driscoll, it offers a fascinating overview of an art which, as O'Driscoll makes plain in his introduction, is nothing if not slippery when it comes to definitions. There is something here for everyone, you would think, in pronouncements that range from the philosophical to the polemical and the aphoristic, and which include such topics as prosody, criticism, anthologies and translation. 'Poetry,' suggests Yves Bonnefoy, 'is an act by which the relation of words to reality is renewed'. 'What is not memorable, in either a deep or simple sense, is not poetry', asserts Edna Longley. From Octavio Paz comes the notion that 'poets talk about the central questions, from a marginal point of view'. 'Opera and poetry are élitist and obscure by nature, and ought to be sold on the joy of difficulty', states Lavinia Greenlaw, while Kathleen Raine believes that 'it is in battling with life and tasks that one becomes a fit person to speak in poetry. A poet must in some way engage with the world. I don't think an ivory tower is a good place to write poetry.'

A number of these statements, like many others in the book, raise as many questions as they attempt to answer. This may have something to do with reading them out of their contexts: what precisely is the 'reality' to which Bonnefoy refers? What kind of battle with life and tasks renders someone 'a fit person to speak in poetry' (a phrase with an echo of 'speaking in tongues')?

The liveliness and range of the debate about what poetry is make it easy to forget that this has been going on for centuries, one way or another. Living in the slipstream of Romanticism, as perhaps we do more than we care to think, may give the discussion a particular edge. As Louis MacNeice put it in his 'Epitaph for liberal poets', a poem more notable for its attitude than its articulation:

> Conditioned to think freely, how can we
> Patch up our broken hearts and modes of thought
> in plaster
> And glorify in chromium-plated stories
> Those who shall supersede us and cannot need us –
> The tight-lipped technocratic Conquistadores?

And that juxtaposition of 'conditioned' and 'freely' also calls to mind the prayerful injunction at the close of Auden's poem in memory of Yeats: 'In the prison of his days / Teach the free man how to praise.'

What does seem still to be needed, even in our age of vehement relativities, is a testing of the whole idea of value. It is this, more than any other issue, which underlies many of the declarations gathered in the Bloodaxe book. It is also the central feature of John Carey's enjoyable book *What Good are the Arts?* (Faber, 2005), an extended squib which breezily defines as a work of art 'anything that anyone has ever considered a work of art, though it may be a work of art only for that one person.' This turns out to be an amazingly easy position to defend, *vis-à-vis* any concept of high art, with the chapters in the book's first part setting up one after another aunt sally to knock down, as their headings suggest: 'Is "high" art superior?'; 'Can science help?'; 'Do the arts make us better?'; 'Can art be a religion?' Each of these is a question expecting, and getting, the answer 'no'. From Kant to Hitler, George Steiner to John Paul Getty, from the 'Mandarin aesthetes' of the Arts Council to art-lovers apparently unaware of or indifferent to global poverty, the targets at which Carey aims his arrows are manifold.

Not everything is negative: he sees popular art as an attempt 'to restore the cohesion of the hunter-gatherer group', and he writes convincingly of the role of the arts in improving the self-respect of those in prison. He also wants everyone in schools to 'experience the arts'. Yet his argument threatens not only the baby along with the bathwater, but the entire fabric of the house. It depends crucially, as he himself admits, on his conviction that we cannot know the sum of individual responses to a work of art. These are, by definition, shut away in other people's consciousness, he maintains, therefore we cannot really know even a single artwork. And of course if the individual is entirely isolated, there can be no agreed sense of 'value'. At one point he does allude to John Stuart Mill's idea of consensus as a way of ascribing value to art, but dismisses it as nothing more than head-counting, which would result in pop music emerging as superior to classical music, or football to sculpture. (The fact, though, is that human beings are not hermetically sealed units: they discuss, they argue, they compare opinions, they come to conclusions, including some about value.)

Having cleared the ground in the first part of his book, in the second Carey changes tack and makes a case for the superiority of literature over other art forms. He defines it as 'writing that I want to remember – not for its content alone ...but for itself: those particular words in that particular order'. Coleridge would have nodded approval. Carey highlights literature as the only art able to reason, to criticise itself, even to moralise. It stocks the mind, and appeals to the imagination by what he characterises as its essential indistinctness: indeed, it liberates the individual reader's imagination. Much here seems beyond dispute, though it is not clear why reason and critical discussion shouldn't be brought to bear on other art forms. And it seems odd not to give weight to the point that there are some experiences which music, or for that matter sculpture or painting, can recapture or evoke more powerfully than words. In any case, Carey comes close to exploding his view of the isolated individual consciousness when attempting to answer his own question, stated as 'how, in this relativist world, one decides which artists or writers or musicians to pay attention to.'

How does the second decade of the 21st century bear out or contradict what Carey has to say, when it comes to pleasure and value? Amid the welter of attitudes and the kinds of antagonisms suggestive of overcrowding in the laboratory, it's possible to discern an assortment of trends, some more encouraging than others. One source of pleasure might be, for a start, the sheer variety of what clusters under the heading of poetry, not least the relatively new prominence of a whole range of idioms taking their place alongside standard English. But why are the differences between, say, poetry aimed at stage performance and poetry written for the quiet of the page sometimes set against one another? There are many houses in the mansion of poetry. As James Fenton, whose poems seem increasingly important, puts it in 'The Manila Manifesto', 'This is no time for people who say: this, this, and only this. We say: this, and *this*, and *that* too.' Incidentally, on the page facing this declaration a two-liner headed *An Amazing Dialogue* goes like this:

> 'But this poem is not like that poem!'
> 'No, you are right, it's not.'

Perhaps it is always the case that successive generations think their own time to be more convulsive than preceding ages, and rarely for the better. In this seesaw reckoning, standards are thought to go down as surely as inflation goes up. The disabused view of Kathleen Raine, writing in *P. N. Review*, sums up this kind of perspective:

> In the course of my lifetime, poets have ceased to be seen as masters of a great art, speaking in the name of some vision of beauty or wisdom. Poetry is something everybody writes, interchangeable, demotic, involving neither skill nor knowledge but only a sufficiently strong urge to write it.

This championing of the art and its craft has a dyspeptic loftiness against which the *Zeitgeist* has set its face, though not entirely: poets such as Geoffrey Hill and J.H. Prynne still speak for the uncompromising complexity that is one of poetry's real redoubts. Yet there is, too, a general sense that poetry is no longer the preserve of an élite. Along with this, there is the increase in the number of creative writing courses; the great efflorescence of translations (witness the achievements of the periodical *Modern Poetry in Translation*, founded by Ted Hughes and Danny Weissbort, and brilliantly sustained by its subsequent editors, David and Helen Constantine); and the establishment of high profile awards such as the T. S. Eliot and the Forward Prizes.

For the most part, however, these are ambiguous gifts. Writing courses may be a perfectly good way of teaching the craft of the art, but can no more make good poets of non-poets than postgraduate certificates can make inspired teachers of non-teachers. Prizes may give great encouragement to individuals, but sometimes at the expense of putting others in the shade: they may even mislead poets away from the development of their natural gift, by seductively inviting mere repetition of a winning formula. Translation broadens our acquaintance with the work of important poets, but it can also be the work of monoglot translators reliant upon literal versions provided by someone familiar with the original language. Too often this results either in that strange no-man's-lingo, translationese, or a text comparable with the one of which Borges said that 'the original is not true to the translation'. On the other hand, you could well argue that courses, prizes and translation offer real opportunities for emerging writers to make their mark.

Perhaps the most serious of Kathleen Raine's charges is

that only the urge to write poetry is required in order to do so. On one level, there seems nothing wrong with this – why shouldn't everyone have a go? On the other hand, you know what she means: it's an attitude towards writing which might be called the Millennium Dome view of poetry. You want to be a Poet, with a capital P. This is the decision you take: this is to be the structure of your life, and its meaning. To invert Eliot, you have the meaning: all you need now is the experience, in the form of some poems to display inside the structure. Maybe some funding would help, too, though no apprenticeship will be required.

It is possible to discern, as one underlying force here, the still striking respect for the whole concept of poetry as memorable utterance – a respect much broader than the sales figures for the great majority of poets would suggest. But another, more insidious factor might be that there is now what looks like a career path for the emerging poet. You follow your creative writing course; you enter prestigious competitions in the hope of winning a prize; you review; you apply for a residency; you keep at the back of your mind the dark but dazzling notion of celebrity. Returning for a moment to American immigration formalities, enter the ghost of Oscar Wilde, that supreme proto-celebrity, with nothing to declare but his genius... Wisława Szymborska, the Polish poet awarded the Nobel Prize in 1996, has some good advice (included in *The Bloodaxe Book of Poetry Quotations*) for those setting out:

> The fear of straight speaking, the constant, painstaking efforts to metaphorise everything, the ceaseless need

to prove you're a poet in every line: these are the anxieties that beset every budding bard. But they are curable, if caught in time.

What I find particularly intriguing in contemporary attitudes is the way in which the perceived gap between mind and heart, sentiment and sentimentality, seems to have widened: or was it always there, only the highlighting varying from age to age? It's a split that divides cleverness from feeling, technical skill and formality from openness of expression. Viewed oppositionally, no approach escapes. Cleverness is perceived as desiccation, irony as defensiveness. Feeling is nothing better than lush self-indulgence or therapy; technical expertise straitjackets the soul and implies too orderly a sense of containment and closure in a fragmented world; playfulness is frivolity; sincerity, when paraded in a poem, is either an embarrassment or plainly insincere. In this perspective, works which bridge the gap, for instance Douglas Dunn's *Elegies* (Faber, 1985), a fine collection written in memory of his first wife, are wrongly seen as, at best, rule-proving exceptions.

Events such as Princess Diana's death and funeral have shown the extent to which we have arrived at the point where sentiment and slush combine. Everywhere it was said with flowers, pile upon sweetly rotting pile of them shrouded in cellophane and heaped around war memorials and other focal points, along with soft toys and poems in weatherproof plastic folders. Poems of unimpeachable sincerity and, *pace* Carey, no poetic value whatsoever, but which still said something about the expectations we have of poetry, and how it fits into many people's perception of feeling and its expression.

I encountered a striking version of such expectations when I was in Bosnia shortly after the end of the war there, at a time when the British Council was considering restarting a literature programme. Among the places where I read was Banja Luka, in the Republika Srpska. The room in which the reading took place was allegedly directly beneath the one occupied by Radovan Karadžić up to the time of his going into hiding. The atmosphere was, if not downright hostile, somewhat tense, with an audience that included several uniformed members of IFOR, the Nato force. From the front row came an early question: 'Why are there soldiers here? Their business is not poetry, but killing'. Not a hard question to answer, given Homer, and poetry's abiding interest in the humanity or otherwise of creatures in or out of uniform. But for the questioner, this indistinction was unacceptable.

And then, there has surely never been an age of such instant and vivid communication as ours. When it comes to knowing about disaster and deprivation, the world is indeed too much with us. There are those who, sometimes for good, sometimes for bad reasons, or simply as a consequence of their temperament, shut out the clamour, but for many it is impossible to remain impervious, even if there is little that we can do individually to make a difference. It is one thing to argue, quite logically, that simple empathy is no good to anyone: quite another to ignore global poverty, natural disasters, or the effects of climate change. Nor is it just a matter of communications: we have seen – still see, all too clearly, the damage and dangers of absolutist thinking, notably in its proselytizing mode. For most people the template of faith, distorted by fanaticism, is no longer a convincing explanation or a credible consolation.

For artists as much as anyone else, this is a matter both of conscience and of consciousness. As John Carey puts it at the end of his book, 'In a world that contains millions of starving people, it is offensive to proclaim that art is as necessary as food.' Brecht made a similar point in his *Dreigroschenoper*: 'Erst kommt das Fressen, dann kommt die Moral'. Grub first, then morality. And the conundrum has its equivalent in the realm of personal misfortune, too. In both spheres it's worth considering Mark Doty's contention (quoted in *The Bloodaxe Book of Poetry Quotations*) that 'the poem that refuses to risk sentimentality, that refuses to risk making a statement, is probably a poem that is going to feel lukewarm.'

A thread that runs through much of the discussion, if not always acknowledged, is the issue of memorability, traditionally seen as one of the prime markers of good poems, and sustained by rhyme and rhythm. It may be easy to exaggerate the predominance, today, of the image over the word, but the reach of the image is surely undeniable, with its ability to lodge vividly in the mind, as well as to cross frontiers. The Czech poet Miroslav Holub made the point that, at a time when his poems were unlikely to be published in his own country, he was inclined to choose his subjects with an eye to their translatability. Probably his best known poem, 'The Fly', is indeed a stark instance of the vivid image, with its horrible but unforgettable picture of the battle of Agincourt, where the fly settled 'on the blue tongue / of the Duke of Clervaux', and then

> she began to lay her eggs
> on the single eye
> of Johann Uhr,
> the Royal Armourer.

Incidentally, these lines (here in a translation by George Theiner) nicely show the role that wit can play in a poem's success without in any way reducing it to mere cleverness.

Conversely, nowadays the use of rhyme and too regular rhythm is seen by some as a sure sign the writer has run aground in the shallows. This may be – but the fact is that many contemporary poets delight in the subtlest of slant, internal and pararhymes, and many continue to exploit or adapt traditional forms with dexterity. Think of the sonnet – a matter not of survival, but of continuing good health.

The short lyric poem in general has proved a doughty survivor, even though its demise is often announced by those who consider it altogether too cosy for our time. A frequent criticism is that its context is often the natural rather than the urban world, though the urban lyric has had no trouble in finding space of its own. Even those who concede that it may still be apt for a world in which both time for reading and our attention span are said to be limited, question its worth. They do so by deploying against it one of the great buzz-words of our contemporary culture, 'relevance'. 'Irrelevant' has become a simple term of dismissal. Often it is used on its own, without any attempt to define a relationship: not 'irrelevant to' something, just irrelevant. Often it appears as a stand-in for some notion of social or political awareness, wielded as a way of demonstrating a good conscience or pacifying a bad one. This is not to say that our age hasn't thrown up new and distinct questions – among them how, if at all, the nature poem might come to terms with such issues as climate change and global warming.

Novelty and originality may also make a poem memorable, up to a point, though too great a preoccupation with this can do an injustice to what has gone before. You can't uninvent the achievements of the past, nor can you kid the public, for much longer than it takes for money to change hands, that well tested techniques and skills axiomatically no longer have a place. James Fenton makes a good point when he writes that 'poetry will wither on the vine if you don't regularly come back to the simplest fundamentals of the poem: rhythm, rhyme, simple subjects – love, death, war'. This is, you might say, the shock of the old. Not that Fenton is in any way a reactionary: on the contrary. He can commandeer the ballad and the near-nonsense poem as easily as the lyric, and his work encompasses love poems, others arising from his time as a war correspondent, and many that display a manic energy and playfulness. Here the arcane rubs tellingly up against the apparently naïve, as it does against the brutal ways of the world: and does so in pulsing, driving rhymes and rhythms which bring words near to the limits of sense. Fenton's take on life – and it is highly effective as a strategy for poems – is that of a genuinely funny clown whose grin not only fails to mask despair, but actually emphasises it. In Fenton's poems, order is a form of hyper-ventilation that knows all about anarchy. Here is an indeed memorable riposte to Dr Johnson's low estimation of wit.

It's not obvious how the faculty of memory might itself develop or atrophy in the age of the computer, and with the oncoming prospect of the e-reader. Why learn by heart when you can conjure, cut and paste, redo or delete at will? As it is, conning by rote is already thought of by the young as being as quaint an activity as the expression suggests. For an older generation, learning by heart may evoke tedious classroom recitations of the Assyrian coming down like the wolf on the fold, dirty British coasters or the gathering of rosebuds while ye may. Yet learning by heart, the inward digestion of a poem, has consequences for our understanding of the text, or at least the place it occupies not in our intellectual understanding, but that nexus where mind and feeling conjoin. Memorising involves what Ted Hughes, in his introduction to the anthology *By Heart: 101 Poems to Remember* (Faber, 1997), refers to as 'the audial memory', which he sees as linked to 'the subsoil of psychological life, beyond our immediate awareness or conscious manipulation'.

When it comes to weighing élitism and populism, pleasure and value, public and private, mind and heart, the process is made more complicated by the sheer volume of work being produced, in a whole variety of Englishes. You'd think this is a situation in which the work of the critic would be of particular use and interest, in guiding a reader through the tangling undergrowth. So it is, with the best critics: the trouble is that they are something of an endangered species.

It is commonly said that the trouble with poetry criticism

is that it is all too often written by poets, friends or enemies of the writer under consideration. Not that there is anything new in this, witness Coleridge's *Anima Poetae*:

> The question should be fairly stated, how far a man can be an adequate, or even a good (so far as he goes) though inadequate critic of poetry, who is not a poet, at least *in posse*. Can he be an adequate, can he be a good critic, though not commensurate? But there is yet another distinction. Supposing he is not only not a poet, but a bad poet! What then?

The nature of poets, Horace's 'touchy tribe', is to be reckoned a factor, and it's certainly true that the spleen of poets can be impressive, and likely to exhibit the vices characteristic of the miniverse of poetry – coterie collusion, hostility based on vanity, or the obsessive settling of old scores. T. S. Eliot, in *The Function of Criticism* (1923), notes just this prevalence of warfare and irrationality. Even so, his succinct definition of the task of the critic looks straightforward enough: it is, he asserts, 'the elucidation of works of art and the correction of taste'. We might choose not to go along with the second half of this phrase, bearing in mind that Eliot maintains elsewhere (in his contribution to a 1935 symposium, *Faith that Illuminates*) that 'literary criticism should be completed by criticism from a definite ethical and theological standpoint'. The rather uncertain nature of Eliot's own thinking is apparent from his oscillation between the idea of an authoritative critical consensus, which he seems reluctant to throw out, and an acknowledgement of the critic's subjectivity that comes close to what John Carey has to say about artistic judgements.

You can see, with both Eliot and Carey, the canyon which is being skirted: if the critic is incapable of objectivity, and his work inevitably solipsistic, there can hardly be much of a place for literary criticism or, for that matter, those who earn their living by it. A further edge of this opening onto air is suggested by another of James Fenton's declarations in *The Manila Manifesto*: 'We despise terrorist normative critics.'

Let's stick with Eliot's word 'elucidation': to cast light upon the nature of the work, to tell the reader about its form and its scope, seems a modest enough ambition. As does some indication, insofar as they may be discernible, of the intentions of the writer – though as many have pointed out, Housman and Eliot among them, the effect of a work of art may not be the one intended by its maker. On the other hand, discerning something of the artist's aim can surely be helpful, preventing the critic from haranguing a bowler hat for not being a top hat, so to speak, and allowing room for the possibility of respecting the work while not actually liking it. I don't see, really, how there can be any worthwhile criticism without such a possibility.

I've only fairly recently caught up with three outstanding collections – Jo Shapcott's *Of Mutability* (Faber, 2010), Christopher Reid's *A Scattering* (Areté Books, 2009) and Helen Dunmore's *The Malarkey* (Bloodaxe Books, 2012). Each of these, in its distinct way, occupies equally and without compromise the realm of human feeling and that of artistic making, like Dunn's *Elegies*. I've also had the chance to review (for *The Warwick Review*) four first collections (by

Nancy Gaffield, Ahren Warner, Eoghan Walls and Judy Brown). Here there is heartening evidence of remarkable variety and intelligence, alongside a wrought quality that suggests we may be on the threshold of an esoteric new *préciosité*.

According to Edwin Morgan, 'Poetry is a brilliant vibrating interface between the human and the non-human.' Perhaps ultimately it is this which guarantees its staying power. Somehow it is in the nature of poetry, most portable of the arts, to be able to exist almost independently of the assorted paths down which we pursue it. Somehow the centre re-forms, and perhaps there are times when exploring the vacated middle ground can start to look more truly radical than some attenuated version of the *avant-garde*. But Louis MacNeice's fears for the fate of the liberal poet have stayed too: for instance, in the later work of a more recent Northern Irish poet, Derek Mahon. The closing verses of the poem 'St Patrick's Day' with which he concludes his *Collected Poems* (Gallery Books, 1999) look to be heading for a letting go reminiscent of Prospero abjuring his 'rough magic':

> I now resign these structures and devices,
> these fancy flourishes and funny voices
> to a post-literate, audio-visual realm
> of uncial fluorescence, song and film,
> as curious symptoms of a weird transition
> before we opted to be slaves of fashion
> – for now, whatever our ancestral dream,
> we give ourselves to a vast corporate scheme

> where our true wit is devalued once again,
> our solitude remembered by the rain.

And then the next, and final, stanza rounds to a mood altogether more philosophical and optimistic:

> The one reality is the perpetual flow,
> chaos of complex systems; each generation
> does what it must; middle age and misanthropy,
> like famine and religion, make poor copy;
> and even the present vanishes like snow
> off a rope, frost off a ditch, ice in the sun –
> so back to the desk-top and the drawing board,
> prismatic natural light, slow-moving cloud,
> the waves far-thundering in a life of their own,
> a young woman hitching a lift on a country road.

It's not too fanciful, I think, to see that young woman of the last line as, on one level, emblematic of the muse – still trusting herself to the open road, game to cross any number of frontiers with her conjuror's suitcase, and still improbably youthful precisely because she, herself, has nothing to declare.

THE CHALLENGE

A visit to Kettle's Yard, in Cambridge – from the outset, it might be the extrapolation of a dream, one very like a fairytale. You arrive at a house that has something secretive about it, though it is impossible to say exactly in what way. It doesn't appear to be made of gingerbread. There is no sign of a bottle standing on a table, filled with a potion which might make you taller or smaller. To the right of the closed door, there is simply a bell-rope to be pulled. And as you will know when you return for further visits, which is very likely to be the case, you have only to ring, and after a short pause someone always appears to let you in.

As with Dr Who's Tardis, what you might have comprehended from the exterior as you approached bears no relation to the nature or dimensions of the inside. You find yourself not in a space, or even a series of spaces, so much as an interspace. How could you define it? Hardly by its name: 'Kettle's Yard' conceals the nature and purposes of the house in the way that some titles of poems decline to tell the reader what the poem is about. You can sketch its character roughly with negatives or partial truths, without being much the wiser. As Jim Ede said, whose house this was, it is not a museum. What museum is as free of labels and explicatory text as this place? Nor is it, quite, a gallery. How many galleries are adorned with fresh flowers in almost every room, or hang their pictures in such domestic settings as a bathroom or lavatory? Nor is it simply the evidence of one man's taste but rather, according to the man himself, 'a continuing way of life'. He also wanted the house to be more than a reflection of 'the taste of a given period'. On one level its interest is of course just that, yet the continuance of Kettle's Yard beyond the lifetime of its founder appears to prove him right: the interspace is temporal as well as spatial. And this impression is heightened by the way in which successive visits bring recognition and growing familiarity but also, always, objects and juxtapositions noticed properly for the first time. It is a bit like walking into that nexus of the moment and the timeless embodied in Eliot's *Four Quartets*.

It's a place that easily defeats attempts at adequate description, if only because it is so easy to omit one or other essential component of its character: and perhaps there is something oneiric about this, too. Nothing here is dissociated, or subject to a change of tense, not even the most secretive part of the house, the attic, with its warm gloaming like a shed in summer and, even though it is under the roof, also the deep-down sense of being somewhere below deck in an old wooden ship. Everything is conjoined in a totality, in associations of texture and light. Within this integrity, there is also the honouring of each singular object, the quiddity of each constituent part: yet nothing is roped off, or made into a precinct. Perhaps most unusually of all, though the lives of the artists whose pictures and sculptures and books make up the ensemble bear witness to their share of human struggle and sadness, there is nothing elegiac in the atmosphere. In the same way, the empty chairs, the china no longer used, the divan bed unrumpled – all are free of ghosts, while keeping somehow a sense of the actual and the particular that no museum-piece can ever quite retain. In many ways being here feels much more like being out of doors than in a confined interior: the affinities are with uncluttered landscapes, with landmarks intensified by the natural light that comes and goes around them, with the wildnesses of the sea.

You wander freely: you could be at a loss, though there are benign guardians who will point you in the right direction, or give information if you require it. They are at their best when they hover silently, available but not insistent. There is so much to take in, so much that claims you – the grain of wood, the shapes and patterns of pebbles arranged in a coil of punctuation, the polished energy of sculpted stone, Alfred Wallis's sailing boats and trawlers pitching in seas where the submerged fish loom like lost souls, the hieratic obliquities of David Jones's multi-layered paintings, Gaudier-Brzeska's bird swallowing a fish, Ben Nicholson's explorations of space and light. And everywhere those vases of flowers, never overblown, entirely without panache, more like posies gathered on an afternoon walk than anything more formal.

You find your way at your own pace, from small ground floor rooms up a narrow stair to a roomier first floor: then up to and down from the attic, before discovering the broader spaces of the extension. In doing so, you undertake a progress that might be said to mirror what Robert Frost wrote about the figure a poem should make – one that begins with delight and ends in wisdom. But you only become aware of this as you leave Kettle's Yard, when you look out across the threshold or when, later, you think back to your visit. You begin to see how much perception depends on context. What you have taken out with you is not just what Jim Ede called 'a continuity of enjoyment', but the notion of continuity in itself. It is as if, having experienced an ideal space in which art and nature might co-exist on equal terms, you are challenged now to seek expressions of its name in the world outside.

PLAYING IT SAFE

In 1956, as a thirteen-year old in a household of three where I was the only male, I found being sent away to boarding school a real shock. In the first weeks the only sensible thing seemed to be to try and grasp the routines, not to fall foul of anyone, and to work out the safest thing to do: safe in the sense of self-protective. I would have benefited from Ovid's advice, which I encountered a few months later: *In medio tutissimus ibis* ('you go most safely in the middle way'). Perhaps because of the circumstances in which I first read it, I have always interpreted this as an argument in favour of camouflage: a way of being inconspicuous and not catching the eye of the auctioneer. Whether that middle constituted compromise or crux was a different matter.

•

Before that, I suppose I must have come across the word 'safety' in two childhood contexts. There were things called 'Safety Matches', made by Bryant & May, and housed in a rickety little box. Their purpose was clear enough, but I didn't quite understand the 'Safety' bit, especially as my sister and I were frequently told that matches were dangerous and could set fire to things (the common adult fault of adding to allure by admonition). You'd have thought we already had a reputation as junior arsonists. Or was it that *these* Bryant & May matches, with their dull purple-brown heads, were indeed safe, while the other Bryant & May matches, cerise-headed and in a box labelled 'England's Glory', with an attractive drawing of a sailing-ship, were the dangerous ones?

Then there were the sheep. Not just any old sheep, but the ones in the hymn, along with their lambs: 'Loving shepherd of thy sheep, / Keep thy lambs in safety keep'. The second line was a bit of a puzzle (were the adult sheep excluded?), but you got the gist. Even if, as Christ and Æsop both warn, a sheep might turn out to be something altogether less innocuous, a camouflaged wolf.

Actual safety, as opposed to just the word, was there from early on: first, in the smell of your mother's skirt, then in the chasing games you played with your friends, in which safety was called 'home' or 'pax'. But the trouble with safety is that, as children know, it quickly becomes boring. Something in the human spirit baulks at it, and at the maxims designed to work in its favour. 'Discretion is the better part of valour'. 'Better safe than sorry'. 'Fore-warned is fore-armed'. 'A stitch in time…'. Was there no end to the wagging of the finger? And what was the point of deadly safety, when all the excitement, the quick of it, lay in the giddiness of taking risks? Thinking of the man who recently crossed above the Niagara Falls on a high wire, doesn't our view of the feat alter once we know that he was wearing a safety harness? On the other hand, to see wingsuit jumpers leaping into the void, for example on Le Brévent above Chamonix, is to be aware of the mortal risk they are taking far more than of the small parachute attached to them – an awareness increased by seeing the words 'Soul Flyer' written on one suit, and by the mournful 'au revoir' uttered by one jumper before taking the plunge. You feel that 'adieu' might have been a more accurate reflection of his closeness to the edge.

For the adolescent, risk-taking in one way or another is almost the norm, a propensity for trying it on based (sometimes lethally) on a super-confident belief in personal immunity from disaster. The approach is not unlike that summoned by T.S. Eliot in his introduction to Baudelaire's *Journaux Intimes* (1930): 'The worst that can be said of most of our malefactors, from statesmen to thieves, is that they are not men enough to be damned. Baudelaire was man enough for damnation…'. Really, it's amazing that so many of us have survived.

As a slightly far-fetched corollary to their habitual reserve, the British used to associate what was dashingly called 'the spirit of adventure' with a kind of amateur casualness predicated on ill-fitting khaki shorts and lightweight plimsolls, the sort of thing you'd wear for climbing Everest: there was thought to be something unmanly and namby-pamby about special kit, let alone precautions and an overdose of planning. Perhaps it was this very licence given to chance and chanciness that prolonged the death-throes of the Empire, being almost impossible to oppose in any calculated way. Certainly it goes with a certain boyish bloody-mindedness. Tell someone for long enough that a given feat is impossible, and they'll have to try it.

Al Alvarez, in his essay 'Risk' (included in *The Penguin Book of 20th Century Essays*, edited by Ian Hamilton, 1999) writes convincingly from the twin viewpoints of the poker player and mountaineer: 'Risk concentrates the mind, sharpens the senses and, in every way, makes life sweeter by putting it, however, briefly, in doubt.' For Alvarez, this produces an unforgettable adrenalin high.

Assessing a risk, when that is possible, involves rational debate: but taking a risk may be more instinctive. At that juncture is it possible really to foresee the consequences of getting it wrong? Is it possible to know one's death beforehand, in the sense of imagining the reality of it? Doesn't the imagination fail at this point, or at any rate tend to romanticize?

Safety, or at least the avoidance of danger, might be instinctive too. In Cyprus, in the summer of 1962, I was trying to sleep, folded uncomfortably into the back of an old Peugeot at Salamis, by the seashore. A stiflingly hot night. I eventually dozed off, lulled by the wavelets flopping softly to land nearby. But then I woke up in a muck sweat, my heart racing, with an imperative certainty that I must get out of there. As I careered back down the track that I had followed a few hours earlier, the headlights showed a figure coming towards me: he stood into the trees at the verge as I went by. Can I really have read in a newspaper later that day about a murderer on the loose in the area, as I think I did? I'm no longer sure – but at the time the urge to get away was powerful enough for me to return the car to the place I had hired it from, and fly back to Beirut a day earlier than I had intended.

Times change. Nowadays, with the potential risk of litigation to hone our awareness of actual risks, any possible looming threat has to be anticipated. I've been asked to fill in a risk assessment form before tutoring a writing course: presumably the organisers would have checked the sharpness of the pencils. As for kit, no one objects to the now long established wearing of safety belts in cars, or helmets for cyclists. At the same time, an amazing accumulation of stuff is marketed as safety equipment, some at least of which looks more like canny retailing than essential lifesaving.

When it comes to children, in the age of the internet, online grooming and all too well publicised instances of abuse, understandable anxieties call the tune. For their safety, we hem children in, doing our best not to give them either an exaggerated or inadequate impression of what the risks might be. For the security of our home, we lock doors and windows and have a house alarm.

Beyond the zone of personal choice and control, safety has assumed grimmer forms, such as the need to guard against radiation leaks from a nuclear power station, or a terrorist bomb, insofar as possible. Think how often it is said of victims of an accident or an atrocity that 'they were just in the wrong place at the wrong time'. That seems impossible for any assessment to ward off.

•

One major compensation for being at boarding school was that my housemaster, Laurence May, was a sympathetic and understanding man. He had a real shyness, which caused him to bury his head in his chest and turn bright red; an extremely fast walking pace, as if to minimise contact or get out of the spotlight as soon as possible; and a delightful tendency to come out with malapropisms of one kind or another. These were enjoyed so much that they were lovingly recorded in an exercise book, or books – there were three by my time. Once you were attuned to them even borderline instances became comic, such as his remark that he had spent the summer holidays at the bottom of Lake Geneva. Others were more centre field, such as 'Don't count your foxes before you face them', or his admonition to a boy that if he once again wrote to a girl in a nearby convent school, 'I shall be in touch with my friend the Virgin Mother'; or his criticism of the school tennis courts as 'not having enough runway'. So it wasn't altogether a surprise when, having concluded an inspection of the boys' genitals with the aid of a torch, to make sure no fungal infections were lurking (a ritual that took place at the start of each term, and involved him walking very fast – probably too fast to fulfil the purpose of his inspection – past each bed in the dormitory, we having lowered our pyjama trousers. It was no good either for his shyness or our modesty), he turned in the doorway before going out and, perhaps in order to conceal his considerable embarrassment and relief that the thing was done, or by way of justification, announced: 'Better to be safe than sure.' It sounded about as safe as you could get.

THE KEY TO CLOVER

It is sometimes hard to gauge the impact of a gift, particularly when the recipient is a child. Even small children can wonderfully and disconcertingly defeat a donor's expectations by, for instance, showing greater interest in the wrapping or box than the present itself. When I was quite young an unhappy cousin gave me a book of Klee reproductions for my birthday. I was captivated and intrigued. One picture especially, from 1927, took hold: *Flagged Town*, a watercolour on paper with a black background. Beneath a looming night sky where, centrally, the solid D of a pale yellow half-moon abuts the stop of a tiny rust-red sun, six flags and pennants arranged in two rows of three dance awry on the towers of a town. These, and other buildings and rooftops, are shown as finely etched outlines, in a kind of crammed diagram. The overall effect, of a tottering settlement, is both specific and archetypal, possibly ancient or possibly timeless. And those flags suggest a kind of defiance, or at any rate occupation: they are not signals of surrender. In any case, something about the picture, its not being either wholly abstract or representational, seemed to place it oddly out of immediate reach.

A love of Klee's work has stayed with me over a lifetime. In some ways this is a mystery. Of course all good art encourages us to pay proper attention: to revalue. But what is there, after all, in this plethora of childlike figures, fir trees, plants, arrows, pyramids, clown-like faces, theatre grotesques, tesseræ of colour, isolated letters or punctuation?

Mostly they are small pictures (*Flagged Town*, for instance, is only 29.4 x 21.6 cm), highly coloured, many on paper or board, some on canvas fraying at the edges, glued rather than stretched. Their range, in terms of subject and techniques, is impressive: and there are huge numbers of them. How could they be grasped and, taken singly or together, what could they mean? In describing them, commentators have often reached for the vocabulary of occlusion – hieroglyphs, ciphers, patchwork, codes. Or of geometry – grids, diagrams, graphs. As Arnfinn Bø-Rygg writes in 'Thinking with Klee' (In *Paul Klee's Enchanted Garden*, Hatje Cantz, 2008), these pictures are 'a kind of pictorial writing existing somewhere between signs and pictures.'

All codes are a challenge, an invitation to pick the lock, with the code rated by the ease or difficulty of cracking it. But what if there is really no solution, if the thing turns out to be a riddle with no answer, like the Mad Hatter's question about why a raven is like a writing-desk, in *Alice's Adventures in Wonderland*? Or, as is the case with many of Kafka's writings, the code may be basically impenetrable even as it relies on the reader's assumptions about the availability of a solution. Such strategies may risk losing the reader's or viewer's interest, but may also be a way of keeping the eye and mind engaged, a playful ambush. Something of this is suggested by the titles Klee gives his paintings: though many are straightforward (*Landscape with Yellow Birds*; *Departure of the Ships*), others are tangential, allusive or cryptic: they can be as amusing or as unhelpful as we decide (*Analysis of Various Perversities*; *The Light and So Much Else*; *Blue-Bird-Pumpkin*). As with the paintings themselves, it depends on what the viewer brings to them.

The four diaries that Klee kept from 1898 to 1918 (edited by Felix Klee, University of California Press, 1968) contain plentiful material for the seeker after enlightenment. Something of a hotch-potch, they trace the development of his character as well as his art. We learn of his love of music (Bach and Mozart were favourites); of his immaturity (he tore up his fiancée's early letters out of irritation, he said); of his admiration for *Candide*, for which he did illustrations. He combines a youthful zest with an awareness of the world's woes: and he begins to define his interests and ambitions as an artist.

Easily the most vivid of the diaries, and the point at which they really come to life, is the third one, which describes his visit to Tunisia with the painters August Macke and Louis Moilliet in April 1914. Klee was thirty-four. His evocation of the country and, in particular, the town of Kairouan, has the force of a Damascene revelation:

> At first, an overwhelming tumult, culminating that night with the *Mariage arabe*. No single thing, but the total effect. And what a totality it was! The essence of *A thousand and one nights*, with a ninety-nine percent reality content. What an aroma, how penetrating, how intoxicating, and at the same time clarifying. Nourishment, the most real and substantial nourishment and delicious drink. Food and intoxication. Scented wood is burning. Home?

His diary entry for Thursday 16th April makes clear

that this was a seminal experience for him, a moment of recognition as well as discovery. He had found a way in which to fulfil the ambition he had set down in his first diary, to penetrate to the heart of things, not merely to reflect surfaces in the way a camera could:

> I now abandon work. It penetrates so deeply and so gently into me, I feel it and it gives me confidence in myself without effort. Color possesses me. I don't have to pursue it. It will possess me always, I know it. That is the meaning of this happy hour: Color and I are one. I am a painter.

From now on, he would develop his ideas with a new confidence and clarity, which begin already to inform the fourth diary: 'becoming is more important than being', he saw. And although 'the more horrible this world the more abstract our art', it was also true that 'I no longer saw any abstract art. Only abstraction from the transitory remained. The world was my subject, even though it was not the visible world.'

But the visible world was grim enough. Within a few months of the visit to Tunisia, the war had begun – and within weeks Macke had been killed. Later, in March 1916, another painter friend, Franz Marc, was killed at Verdun. As Klee readily admits, his war was very different: the fourth diary relates the endless muddle of it all, the permits and timetables and bureaucracy, the clumsiness and waste: a chaos enlivened by the occasional good meal. Any wider thinking tends to concentrate on the subject closest to him:

'In art,' he writes, 'vision is not so essential as making visible'. And already Kairouan is beginning to assume the status of a somewhat sentimental myth:

> ...if only I might hear again the wonderful duo of the two Tunisian beggars in the quiet, white alley at noon, in front of the locked door! Where the one answered the other and the voices joined for a few measures, and at the end fell away together in such a peculiar, surprising fashion. And right afterward, the door opened slightly, one surmised a figure there and saw a delicate hand holding out a few coins.

Re-reading the diaries after some years, I was struck by two entries on the subject of art (both in the third diary) which seem as pertinent now as when they were written. 'Today,' Klee writes, 'everybody wants to be a unique phenomenon'. And further on: 'Democracy with its semi-civilization sincerely cherishes junk. The artist's power should be spiritual. But the power of the majority is material. When these worlds meet occasionally, it is pure coincidence.' Seen through the blurry filter of some contemporary artists' success, this seems prescient.

Finally, the diaries illuminate the paintings only to a limited extent. And though Klee wrote copiously about his theories and convictions (for instance, in his *Notebooks*), I want to come back to the pictures themselves – to assume the position of the viewer rather than the commentator. I realise that describing pictures with words is a bit like expecting someone to enjoy a television programme by admiring the aerial, but I hope that what follows – a brief tour of some of my favourite Klee pictures that also attempts to convey something of his scope – may incite the reader to discover these and other Klee pictures for him- or herself.

Rose Garden (1920/21), Oil on cardboard, 49 x 42.5 cm

The roses are almost like fingerprint whorls, circular and rigid as microphones on their straight stems. Here is a landscape rather than a garden – and a good instance of Klee's overcoming what he called 'the dead end of ornamentation', though he does so by working through it rather than in direct opposition. Almost fractured by divisions of colour and line, the picture is a composite assembled in a variety of colours – white, pink, madder. Dynamic, mobile, optically tricksy, it presents the setting for the roses as a place of odd redoubts and enclaves that add depth and, in their vertical stances, belie the essentially lateral energies of the landscape. Half camouflaged by colour are towers, gable ends, spires. And, for this viewer at least, there is a presiding feeling of tension and tight enclosure which is not without a sense of threat. If this is a garden, its roses must be as spiky as any stem armed with thorns.

Separation in the Evening (1922), Watercolour, 33.5 x 23.5 cm

Horizontal bands of colour show darkness descending, but lightening from greyish-purple as it goes down to meet the waning earth-light, which itself modifies from light brown to sand as it rises to the oncoming night. Geometric, diagrammatic, the picture seems to show the relationship of different fields of force or pressure. Two vertical arrows (the upper one heading down towards the lower one heading up) play off both against one another and against the horizontal bands. Paradoxically, the arrows pointing towards one another suggests meeting rather than parting. And there's humour in the way they draw attention to the strip at whose edge they stop – the almost central strip (the 5th of 11, counting down), though closer to the bottom of the picture than the top. As if they indicate a meaning or an emphasis beyond that of shifting colour tones: the arrow as sign has its own code of suggestion. This picture has a close affinity with 'Eros', another watercolour of the same period. Here two vertical arrows both point upwards, their pyramidal heads seen within the context of a larger pyramid of shifting colour tones that pierces yet another (smaller) pyramid pointing down from the top of the picture. Nearly identical in size, both pictures call to mind Klee's comment, in his *Notebooks*, that 'The pictorial work springs from movement, it is itself fixated movement, and it is grasped in movement (eye muscles).'

The Goldfish (1925), Oil & watercolours on paper, mounted on board, 48.5 x 68.5 cm

Fish are the perfect embodiment of stillness combined with movement: swimming, stationary or just gliding, borne along by the flow. And fish point a direction almost as much as an arrow. They also inhabit a world that is fecund, rich with animal and plant life; and, in its depths, hidden. Small wonder that such creatures and their context recur in Klee's work, given his liking for what may lie beyond appearances. This large (for Klee) picture is richly coloured: the goldfish, red-eyed, bristling with needle-fine red fins, dominates the centre, while smaller red fishes head away towards the corners of the painting, perhaps trying to escape: and all swim in a rich blue ocean thick with eerily lit plants and growth. There is something dream-like about the luminosity of the fish: it seems to be lit from within.

Deep in the Forest (1939), Mixed media on oil-primed canvas, 50 x 43 cm

The sense of submersion, this time on land, is intense. Never a tree in sight: we are too deep in to see them. Emerald green plants, leaves and uncertain shapes in close-up, dominant, peer out from the background of a slightly darker green. One is a propeller-like bloom on a bending stalk; the shape of another is reminiscent of a sunflower, its seeds held in a fringed circle; others have leaf-like serrations; one, shaped more like a piece of cloth than a plant, stands oddly up on the right. This is mood music, dream-like, all-pervasive and strangely persuasive, fulfilling its own terms. Its depths, though conveyed on a single plane, have an absoluteness due in part to the lack of context: but for the title, we wouldn't know that we were at the heart of a forest, amid intensities of secrecy, of inwardness.

Kettledrummer (1940), Paste colour on paper, mounted on board, 33 cm x 20.3 cm

'The objects in pictures look out at us serene or severe, tense or relaxed, comforting, forbidding, suffering or smiling', Klee wrote in a lecture given in Jena in 1924. Here, painted sixteen years later, is a picture certainly looking at us – grimly, with its staring Cyclops eye. Along with several other paintings from the last years of Klee's life, this is shocking in its brute coarseness, when compared to the delicacy and detail of much of the earlier work: thick black outlines, a minimal scribble of red. Black and red, the colours of death and blood. It is hard to consider this picture without having in mind the war and the Nazi tyranny, as well as Klee's own impending death. But there is no doubting its dramatic effectiveness – the arms themselves have become drumsticks, the glaring head looks like a soldier's helmet. No room for the imaginative forces of generosity or compassion, only the imperatives of force and the summoning drum.

•

> *I cannot be grasped in the here and now. For I live just as well with the dead as with the unborn. Somewhat closer to the heart of creation than usual. And still far from close enough.*
> *(Diesseitig bin ich gar nicht fassbar. Denn ich wohne grad so gut bei den Toten, wie bei den Ungeborenen. Etwas näher dem Herzen der Schöpfung als üblich. Und noch lange nicht nahe genug.)*

These words, included in the catalogue of an exhibition at the Galerie Goltz in Munich, and published in the gallery's house journal *Der Ararat* (May 1920), were to be used as Klee's epitaph. The measure taken here is one of movement across a frontier: in this it chimes perfectly with the presiding spirit of Klee's work, evident even in such apparently simple instances as the 1926 drawing *Migrating fish*. Here it's as if the fish have learned to disguise themselves as waves, as slippage of the light, lithe crests of darkness whose identity is, here and there, suggested as a small eye, the twist of a tail-fin. And their migration? Between the latent and the actual, in moments so bright and silver-quick as to be themselves all and nothing: the sighting of them a matter of faith – and bringing the recognition of a mysterious depth, or some other form of coding, such as the French for key or the German for clover.

> As a result of all my reading and meditation, I abstracted two critical aphorisms, deeming them to comprise the conditions and criteria of poetic style: first, that not the poem which we have read, but that to which we *return* with the greatest pleasure, possesses the genuine power and claims the name of essential poetry. Second, that whatever lines can be translated into other words of the same language without diminution of their significance, either in sense of association or in any worthy feeling, are so far vicious in their diction.

This comes from the opening chapter of Coleridge's *Biographia Literaria*, which finally appeared in two volumes in July 1817, after a long delay that was not only frustrating but financially damaging to the author – and with a large number of misprints. It's a mild enough beginning, and the assertion has often enough been re-made since – that poetry is not what we read, but what we re-read; and that the language of poetry must be heightened in some way, apart from everyday usage. 'News that stays news', as Pound put it.

By chapter two, however, Coleridge's aim becomes more focused: he is gunning for the kind of critic who is a lazy, inattentive reader. Not that he himself would be roused to indignation by the ensuing misjudgements, we are to understand, though 'I deem it a writer's duty, and think it creditable to his heart, to feel and express a resentment proportional to the grossness of the provocation and the importance of the object.' It is no surprise to find that Coleridge himself has been the victim of such sloppiness, as he tells us with what looks like considerable irritation, despite his disclaimer:

> Without any feeling of anger therefore...I may yet be allowed to express some degree of surprize that after having run the critical gauntlet for a certain class of faults which I *had*...I should, year after year, quarter after quarter, month after month...have been for at least seventeen years...forced to abide the brunt of abuse for faults directly opposite, and which I certainly had not. How shall I explain this?

Warming to his theme, he is careful to make clear that his views are not based on envy: any prudent man would give praise where it is due, and rejoice in a fellow writer's earned success. For all that (and he does enjoy his aphorisms, you sense), 'Praises of the unworthy are felt by ardent minds as robberies of the deserving', and 'for as long as there are readers to be delighted with calumny there will be found reviewers to calumniate.'

He goes on to suggest that things will only get worse as literature is ever more widely distributed. This 'shall produce an increase of sciolists; and sciolism bring with it petulance and presumption. In times of old, books were as religious oracles; as literature advanced, they next became venerable preceptors; they then descended to the rank of instructive friends; and as their numbers increased they sank still lower to that of entertaining companions.' 'Sciolist' – 'A superficial pretender to knowledge; a conceited smatterer', according to the Oxford English Dictionary. We all know a smatterer or two.

By now (chapter three) Coleridge is well into his stride. The worthless reviewer, he asserts, is negative in his approach, sure to pick out poems or passages he dislikes, by which 'he wastes as much more paper than the author as the copies of a fashionable review are more numerous than those of the original book'. And until proper critical criteria are established to which reviewers adhere, there will be nothing better than 'arbitrary dictation and petulant sneers' of a kind which no thinking person would respect: 'reflecting minds will pronounce it arrogance in them thus to announce themselves to men of letters as the guides of their taste and judgement.'

This vigorous polemic runs all through the *Biographia Literaria*, the emphases and direction of the argument adjusted here and there. Coleridge never quite succeeds in detaching his own sense of injustice from the quest for objective standards of judgement: he may not have wanted to. Indeed he implies their interconnection when he writes (Chapter 18) that 'the ultimate end of criticism is much more to establish the principles of writing than to furnish rules how to pass judgement on what has been written by others; if indeed it were possible that the two could be separated.' Much of the enjoyable energy of his writing comes from this attempt to protect the worthwhile from the merely chic: a page further on, he declares it 'the prerogative of poetic genius to distinguish by parental instinct its proper offspring from the changeling which the gnomes of vanity or the fairies of fashion may have laid in its cradle or called by its names.' So it becomes a part of the poet's responsibility to separate the wheat from the chaff, since 'the rules of the imagination are themselves the very powers of growth and production. The words to which they are reducible present only the outlines and external appearance of the fruit.' As for the critic, he must declare his hand by announcing his criteria for judgement, allowing the reader to see how they apply to the work under consideration. Once this has been established, all will be well, allowing the critic a proper freedom:

> Every censure, every sarcasm respecting a publication which the critic, with the criticized work before him, can make good is the critic's right. The writer is authorized to reply, but not to complain. Neither can any one prescribe to the critic how soft or how hard, how friendly or how bitter, shall be the phrases which he is to select for the expression of such reprehension or ridicule. The critic must know what effect it is his object to produce; and with a view to this effect must he weigh his words.

As it is (and Coleridge cannot resist returning to the fray), reviews in periodicals are far from satisfactory:

> I am referring to the substitution of assertion for argument; to the frequency of arbitrary and sometimes

> petulant verdicts, not seldom unsupported even by a single quotation from the work condemned, which might at least have explained the critic's meaning if it did not prove the justice of his sentence. Even where this is not the case the extracts are too often made without reference to any general grounds or rules from which the faultiness or inadmissibility of the qualities attributed may be deduced, and without any attempt to show that the qualities *are* attributable to the passage extracted.

He cites reviews of Wordsworth as a case in point, and concludes by advising the author of any newly published poem not to have too great an expectation:

> And first, allowances must be made for private enmity, of the very existence of which they had perhaps entertained no suspicion – or personal enmity behind the mask of anonymous criticism: secondly, for the necessity of a certain proportion of abuse and ridicule in a review in order to make it saleable...

It's remarkable how pertinent Coleridge's criticisms of the critics have remained across a gap of two centuries, as questions about the value of poetry and of the arts in general continue to be asked – by critics, by dispensers of grants and public money, by the public. Amongst the former, one of the most interesting was I. A. Richards, who in his *Principles of Literary Criticism* (1924) addresses precisely the issues raised by Coleridge. For him, 'the two pillars upon which a theory of criticism must rest are an account of value and an account of communication.' In a passage that closely echoes Coleridge's reservations about the greater availability of literature, Richards suggests that greater commercialism has made the need for critical guidance and discrimination even more important:

> To bridge the gulf, to bring the level of popular appreciation nearer to the consensus of best qualified opinion, and to defend this opinion against damaging attacks...a much clearer account than has yet been produced, of why this opinion is right, is essential.

He acknowledges the subjectivity of reading ('It is unquestionable that the actual experiences, which even good critics undergo when reading, as we say, the *same poem*, differ very widely') and is particularly strong on discussing rhythm and expectancy, as well as the comparison to be made between music and language – where he nods explicitly to Coleridge: 'To point out that "the sense of musical delight is a gift of the imagination" was one of Coleridge's most brilliant feats.' Above all, Richards affirms that 'a critic should often be in a position to say, "I don't like this but I know it is good", or "I like this and condemn it", or "This is the effect which it produces upon me, and this quite different effect is the one it should produce."'

Enter T. S. Eliot. *The Use of Poetry and the Use of Criticism*, published in 1933, has its share of Coleridgean shafts, from 'the lazy habit of substituting, for a careful study of the texts, the assimilation of other people's opinions' to the contemporary replacement, as Eliot sees it, of proper, detailed textual consideration by 'a criticism which seems to demand of poetry, not that it shall be well written, but that it shall be "representative of its age".' Like Coleridge, he is aware of the potential for distortion, in the confined world of poetry: 'When the critics are themselves poets, it may be suspected that they have formed their critical statements with a view to justifying their poetic practice.' And he sounds even more like his predecessor when he writes of '...the criticism of persons qualified neither by sensibility nor by knowledge of poetry, from which we suffer daily.'

He had already sounded the same note of discontent in *The Function of criticism* (1923):

> Criticism, far from being a simple and orderly field of beneficent activity, from which imposters can be readily ejected, is no better than a Sunday park of contending and contentious orators, who have not even arrived at the articulation of their differences.

He saw, too, the danger in the critical industry of the proliferation of books about books, while reserving his real censure for those who failed to convey truth, preferring instead their own views:

> Of course the multiplication of critical books and essays may create, and I have seen it create, a vicious taste for reading about works of art instead of reading the works themselves, it may supply opinion instead

> of educating taste. But *fact* cannot corrupt taste … The real corrupters are those who supply opinion or fancy.

So the arguments rumble on, as they always will, with varying degrees of alienation from the way the world is going. For F. R. Leavis (in 'Mass Civilization and Minority Culture') 'the symptoms and causes, the agencies, of decline include the car, the popular press, films, broadcasting (less obviously), advertising (in its effects on the language), arbiters of taste such as Arnold Bennett...'; and the contemporary reader 'is exposed to a concourse of signals so bewildering in their variety and number that, unless he is especially gifted or especially favoured, he can hardly begin to discriminate.' While the small band of the gifted can fend for itself, 'there is a relatively large public that goes for guidance to the *Observer* and the *Sunday Times*' – or rather, Leavis suggests, is at their mercy. As for the *cognoscenti*, they are stranded in an increasingly hostile environment that fends them off with critical terms such as 'worthwhile' and 'highbrow'.

From the poets themselves, there have continued to be interesting contributions – *inter alios*, Randall Jarrell ('The Obscurity of the Poet') and Philip Larkin ('The Pleasure Principle'). Like Leavis, Jarrell sees the dangers for poetry inherent 'in a world whose newspapers and magazines and books and motion pictures and radio stations and television stations have destroyed, in a great many people, even the capacity for understanding real poetry, real art of any kind… Yet one sort of clearness shows a complete contempt for the reader, just as one sort of obscurity shows a complete respect…'

(a viewpoint Geoffrey Hill would surely find congenial). But, unlike Leavis, he believes profoundly in the virtue of the arts being available to all: 'One of the oldest, deepest and most nearly conclusive attractions of democracy is manifested in our feeling that through it not only material but also spiritual goods can be shared: that in a democracy bread and justice, education and art, will be accessible to everybody'. Larkin believes the problems facing poetry arise from 'a cunning merger between poet, literary critic and academic critic (three classes now notoriously indistinguishable)' which has undermined the views of the common reader and resulted in what he sees as predominantly a student audience.

He sees only one hope of amelioration:

> ...a large-scale revulsion has got to set in against present notions, and...it will have to start with poetry readers asking themselves more frequently whether they do in fact enjoy what they read, and, if not, what the point is of carrying on. And I use the word 'enjoy' in the commonest of senses, the sense in which we leave a radio on or off.

I'm not sure this adds much by way of critical guidance, however comforting it may be for the literary equivalent of *l'homme moyen sensuel.* At least it has the virtue of clarity, which cannot invariably be said of the plethora of theories scattered in profusion over the last fifty years, like radar-baffling foil from a plane.

Where are we now? The world has changed a great deal since Richards and Eliot wrote, though sometimes in ways that they anticipated interestingly, as in Richards's picking up on Haldane's ideas about the future:

> The next age but two, if an oncoming Age of Relativity is to be followed as Mr. Haldane supposes by an Age of Biology, will be introduced by a recognition on the part of many minds of their own nature...a recognition which is certain to change their behaviour and their outlook considerably.

And at a time when novelty tends to be given an axiomatic status that it does not always deserve, it's worth remembering what Eliot wrote in *Tradition and the Individual Talent* about the relation of any worthwhile poet to the past: 'No poet, no artist of any art, has his complete meaning alone. His significance, his appreciation is the appreciation of his relation to the dead poets and artists'. And, as Eliot goes on to write, even if novelty is preferable to repetition, each new accretion amends the past as well as altering the future.

Recently the gap between between scholarly criticism and the reviewing of poetry in newspapers and periodicals seems to have widened. It's easy to knock academic reviewing as too specialised, but this is nonsense – who would want to be without, for instance, John Fuller's excellent *W. H. Auden: A Commentary* or Jonathan Bate's *The Genius of Shakespeare*? And the greater presence now of practising writers in the world of the academy must surely be a broadening influence. But, with striking honourable exceptions, the sloppiness of much current poetry reviewing is every bit as bad as that condemned by Coleridge. All too often it simply fails to attend to the work in question. In such writing, there is little evidence that much of the book has actually been read, let alone considered. What is elucidated, though, is the nature of the perpetrator's own intentions: it can seem that the book under review is little more than a platform which the critic mounts in order to proclaim his or her own beliefs. Cleverness is the criterion rather than truth.

Of course all of us, whether as poets or critics, have blind spots and can fail to see the point: but this is hardly an excuse for the exercises in irresponsibility and sloth too often in evidence in the columns of periodicals and magazines. Too many editors seem to think it in order to give reviewing work to interns, or tyros out to make elbow room for themselves: and while the best critics are beyond reproach and continue to offer valuable insights, far too much of the middle ground is occupied by self-interested squealers, barkers and growlers. The situation is not helped by the continuing contraction of the space allotted to poems and reviews, the hastiness induced by tight deadlines or the increasing tendency of periodicals to favour a particular small group of writers. And there is sometimes a complex overlap, not always clearly defined even when legitimate, between literary judgements and those pertaining to citizenship, political rights and other agendas. Equally unhelpful are the strands in our culture that encourage such innovations as The Hatchet Job of the Year prize, whose declared aim is 'to boost the profile of professional arts criticism and make it more accessible and entertaining'. Publicity über alles.

Above all, the language sometimes used in reviewing can be shockingly imprecise, with an overblown affection for the demotic. I've read reviews that take their stand on such startling critical terms as 'Wow!' or 'Yawn!' or even, in one case, 'this is a book that really knocked my socks off!' Fine, if the enthusiasm (or the dismissal) is backed up by genuine critical evaluation: but too often the vehement exclamation stands in for any real thinking or illustration, demanding that the reader take the reviewer's approbation or censure on trust.

In one important way the space for critical discourse has broadened, with the advent of the internet. But as a critical forum it is quite indiscriminate, a place where really interesting and informed comment jostles against off-the-wall ranting, envy and plain misunderstanding. Lively as it is, it too emphasises the need for a more informed and thoughtful consideration of a writer's intentions, and his or her degree of success in achieving them.

Meanwhile, it's worth remembering the critical reception given to *Biographia Literaria* by prominent periodicals of the time such as *Blackwood's*, which was hostile, and the *Quarterly Review*, which chose not to notice it at all. The first edition was the only one to appear in Coleridge's lifetime: I've been reading the fourth, annotated and edited by George Watson (Dent, 1975). Time does its winnowing.

25th February 2012: I wake to a cold clear day and try to bring into focus the excitement I feel. It's the kind of thrill I used to experience as a child when, waking early on Christmas morning, I felt the weight of the stocking across the foot of the bed and, wriggling my toes underneath it, heard its squeaky rustling. But that can't be it: the 25th, it's true, but the wrong month. Then I get it. England versus Wales, and a first return to Twickenham in over forty years, thanks to a friend, Nick Grant, who has generously offered me a ticket. Forget Saint Niklaus.

From far out, the event exercises its centripetal influence. The train from Devon to London is fully booked. You can tell who's going to the match: they chatter like the acolytes of a new revelation; like pilgrims, ecstatic at a range of almost 150 miles. As if everything – the blurred landscape, even – were being sucked in, homing.

On the way, I open the paper at a picture with the caption: 'Children playing with a ball in Jakarta's floodwaters'. Play is such a basic instinct – all it needs is space, markings on the ground; a ball, the angle of a wall. Even in this age of statistics, it may be that no one has yet computed the fraction of the earth's surface given over to sports. And from childhood onwards, from conkers, marbles and hopscotch to tag, playground games, private mind-games and team sports, the human tendency to play games and to compete against self, the clock or others, is clearly established. *Hupane! Kaupane!* (Up the step! A second step!), to quote one of the famous Hakas with which New Zealand All-Blacks rugby teams confront their opponents at the outset. Or the Olympic motto, the hendiatris *Citius*, *Altius*, *Fortius*: 'Faster, Higher, Stronger'.

The variety of sports is truly remarkable, from the sealed interiors of snooker and billiards, to the sunlit shine of the ski slopes, from *pétanque* to tennis, football to fives, sailing to darts, hang-gliding to hockey, gymnastics to golf (even on the moon), horse-racing to rugby, from the great god cricket to the great god football. Sport is everywhere, for better and for worse: in films, on radio and television, in traffic diversions and crowds of rival fans kept apart from one another; even in poetry, despite Yeats's contempt for those who 'run hither and thither in some foolish sport', and Kipling's dismissal of the English as a decadent people who had 'contented their souls / With the flannelled fools at the wicket or the muddied oafs at the goals' (quoted by Ian McMillan in his foreword to *Not Just a Game*, Five Leaves, 2006. He also observes that '... sporting poems...are about human endeavour, about hopes and fears, and about how we construct ways of living with each other and with ourselves.') It's worth remembering that in the early Olympics verse speaking went alongside athletics – last year's Cultural Olympiad seemed an honourable attempt to achieve something of the same.

For many, though, the thought of sport is inseparable from the recall of bitter cold and rain, the dread of failure compounded by the mockery of the onlookers, or the pungent smell of dried sweat and embrocation in dingy changing rooms. Nonetheless, sport *is* everywhere – on the river, the pitch, the greens, in the water, the sky, at the poker tables. Its very ubiquity makes it at least understandable that some should want to hear no more of it. Given that 2012 was the year of the London Olympics, they are spectacularly out of luck.

For some, sport is a calendar and a guide to the past, with a cast that is different for each generation: for mine, it includes Bannister's 4-minute mile (Chataway pacing) at Iffley Road, Oxford; Stirling Moss and Fangio; Donald Campbell and 'Bluebird' (is this sport?); Billy Wright, Stanley Matthews, Pelé, Puskás; Cassius Clay/Ali; Drobny. All men, you note: only relatively recently has the light shone justly on women, as on the remarkable feats of disabled athletes.

Since the earliest days of the tribe, the links between sport, legend and myth have been well established. Hedged about with the record book, almanacs and bar-room reminiscence, sport has even ventured onto the sacred ground of the British weather, reminding us that the race is not always to the swift, nor the battle to the strong. And quite apart from the climate, everyone can recall the day a team of known talent falls flat on its face, under-performing wildly as if succumbing to some unseen barometric lowering of pressure. In this, as in the vicissitudes of the betting common to most sport, it is precisely the element of uncertainty that intensifies the buzz.

Sport is, on one level, a kind of grotesque exaggeration. In the case of British teams, it takes the form of the constant over-hyping of prospects, as if the commentators were operating from the last outpost of Pathé News: as if they were lauding the umpires on which the sun never sets. Condemned thus to disappointment, the public takes refuge in desperate emotional venting, in chants, emblems, replica shirts and rituals.

In the age of television deals, the exaggeration has spread to encompass the public and private lives of participants. The age of big money, too – it's noteworthy that the two most successful teams of the 2011–2012 English football season, Manchester City (Premiership winners) and Chelsea (F.A. Cup winners, European club champions), between them accounted for expenditure and investment in excess of three billion pounds. It would be sad indeed if success were to be calibrated solely according to financial outlay: not exactly a level playing field, to borrow from the commentators' broad repertoire of cliché. And the potential for conflating team support and patriotism has not escaped the advertisers: BACK OUR BOYS AND PLACE YOUR BETS! was the exhortation of a television commercial broadcast during the Euro 2012 football championships.

There is, of course, a price to pay, even for the beneficiaries of sporting money. The rewards, on a par with those achieved by the chief executives of multi-national companies and banks, are counterbalanced by the merciless pressures of exposure. Even – particularly, rather – the blunders of sportsmen are exposed to the world. Few could equal the pictures of the unfortunate goalkeeper of a South American football team who, having safely caught the ball, pirouettes once too often in preparing to throw it to one of his defenders. The ball seems glued to his hand till, freeing itself at precisely the wrong moment, it hurtles into his own net.

When it comes to politics, the record of sport has been erratic, to say the least. On the one hand, it has been a prism through which to focus protest, as in South Africa or Zimbabwe: on the other, it has been a perpetrator of social division and inequality, typically defining exclusive territory reserved for members who qualify by being male, or white, or rich, or any combination of the three. In this respect, full marks to boxing for its inclusiveness and the opportunities it has historically offered to ethnic minorities (last year's Olympic games included, for the first time, women's boxing); likewise to those firms such as Boots, Cadbury, Rowntree, Lyons and Singer, that have in the past seen fit, allbeit with good pragmatic reasoning (a healthy and contented work force is less likely to strike) to provide sports facilities for both female and male employees.

Berlin in 1936 remains in many ways the *locus classicus* of sport and politics getting tangled. But it's also a kind of Æsopean fable in which the malign Aryan ambitions of Hans von Tschammer und Osten, as *Reichssportführer*, and his master are soundly defeated by Jesse Owens and his haul of no fewer than four gold medals (in the 100 metres, 200 metres, long jump, and the 4 x 100 metres relay). Berlin also gave birth to Leni Riefenstahl's inglorious film *Olympia* (1938). However technically impressive, its two parts, *Fest der Völker* (Festival of Nations) and *Fest der Schönheit* (Festival of Beauty) reek of propaganda and a sleek decadence.

And what an irony that the next summer Olympics to be held in Germany, in Munich in 1972 (the stadium was built in a pit made by World War II bombs), should have witnessed the killing of eleven Israeli athletes by Palestinian gunmen. Mindful of Berlin 1936, the West German government, keen to promote a positive image of the new, democratic Germany, had chosen as the games' official motto 'the Happy Games'.

Perhaps one of the best events to have been staged at the Munich Olympiastadion, some years later, was the Monty Python sketch pitting a football team of Greek philosophers against one from Germany. The players include Leibnitz and Plato in goal, Schopenhauer and Sophocles as defenders, with Nietzsche and Archimedes among the forwards. Confucius is the referee, armed with an hourglass (Nietzsche, claiming that Confucius has no free will, is shown a yellow card. Confucius he say 'Name go in book'). You get the idea. Thomas Aquinas and St. Augustine are touch judges: the German manager is Martin Luther. Franz Beckenbauer is the one genuine footballer playing. Socrates scores the only goal of the match, a diving header from a cross by Archimedes. The Germans protest: Hegel maintains that the reality is merely an *a priori* adjunct of non-naturalistic ethics, while Kant deploys the categorical imperative to argue that ontologically it exists only in the imagination. Marx claims it was an offside goal.

And now, with the Beijing games of 2008 having upped the ante breathtakingly in terms of display, scale and expense, it was the turn of London. Rather, of the United Kingdom, witness the route taken by the Olympic torch in advance of the games. It was to be paraded through more than 1,000 cities, towns and villages, the organisers told us, passing 'within an hour of 95 per cent of people in the UK, the Isle of Man, Guernsey and Jersey during the 70-day Torch Relay. It will enable local communities to shine a light on the best their area has to offer'. A brilliant PR stunt, you might think, and so it was – but something more, too. In Exeter, where I live, the torch was to pass a street away from our house, and we strolled across to watch it go by. The crowd was considerable but not oppressive, lining the road to the city centre: the mood was light and positive, with many people chatting or waving to friends. And when, after a wait of some forty minutes, the cavalcade arrived, it was like a less hectic version of the *Tour de France* – but with the same excitement. Near to where we stood, the elderly woman gymnast in a white tracksuit who was to run the next short traverse was dropped from a coach, complete with her golden torch. Then, police motorcyclists, all fluorescent yellow and blue lights, roundly cheered by the crowd: later, police cyclists, one of whom checked the gymnast's torch; then, at last, the flame itself – another white-clad figure, escorted on either side by three runners wearing grey tops and shorts. In their wake, coaches carrying spare runners and escorts, the back-up flame (the 'mother flame' as the official lingo had it, in a quasi-religious mode); other coaches boasting the generosity of sponsors; and, finally, an unruly squad of adults and children on bikes bringing up the rear. The new torch was lit from the old one, and the relay resumed.

All this amounted somehow to more than the sum of its parts. There was a real sense of – well, the simple pleasures of neighbourliness and community, along with the often expressed comment that this was something that would happen 'only once in a lifetime'. For how many causes would such a crowd convene in so many places, let alone as an assemblage of smiles rather than outrage? Not that there was a complete absence of background shadow: the universal prayer had to be that the dark shadow of disruption and terror would stay clear of east London.

Yet even with the weight of historical or political contexts, there is a sense in which any sporting event is isolated in time by being heightened as well as transient, floating clear of any exegesis or computation. When the whistle blows for the start, the intense enjoyment and drama of the occasion can blot everything else out.

Sport and mortality recognise one another: they are allies in the apotheosis of the moment. Every sporting contest takes place on a *campus rasus* of one kind or another – the mown pitch with its green stripes, dazzling white lines, and stiff small flags fluttering at the corners; the pool of light flooding down onto the brushed baize or the chequered board. And each event, like the reading of a book, enacts a journey from ignorance to knowledge.

After the event, the dispersal: the spectators drifting homewards, the arena emptying out. The scrape of polystyrene litter blown along the terraces, the empty seats, the discarded hollowed-out moment. The trains, cars, coaches draw away from the wrapped-round secrecy of the stadium walls. Funnelled into sideroads and subways, the crowd becomes a tide of mere pedestrians. And there comes the thought that any event, however outstanding in the singular splendour of its moment, is pitted against the clock, against time: 'arena', from the Latin *harena*, sand.

Postscript

With the London Olympic and Paralympic games over, it's clear they developed fully the positive spirit evident in the crowds that gathered beforehand to watch the progress of the Olympic flame round the United Kingdom. How this spirit might be sustained or manifest itself in the longer term (for instance in a greater focus on sport in schools) it is too soon to tell.

GNOMES

A

Architecture: for dictators, a form of sentimentality.

Atheists never stop talking about God: believers, about doubt.

B

"Bear with me".
"But I hardly know you…"

Books: place in separate piles the books you have read / the books you got signed by the author / the books you have been given / the books you have borrowed and not returned / the books you have not yet read. Which pile is the tallest, and which the smallest?

C

Childhood: a territory where, since there is only one personal pronoun, there are none.

Climate change: to predict disaster may be the last hope.

D

Darkness and silence: two great tutors, if you can find them.

Death, according to the leaflet enclosed with the tablets, is a rare side-effect: shouldn't we all be taking them by the handful?

E

Eating out: one definition of a good waiter – someone who can make removal of the empty glass, the drained carafe, an act of supreme empathy.

Europe: a place that the British talk of going into, as if there were no such continent where Britain is.

F

Flat screen television: an exact description – the imagination flattened, much of the real world screened off.

Forgetfulness: the art of omitting memory.

G

Generosity: the rain on the catalpa leaves.

Grief: a form of repeated ambush.

H

Happily ever after: written off, dead.

Houdini: with one bound he was free – with two, at a loss.

I

Imagination, individual, instinct, irony, the I of eternity: the pillar on a headland.

Incomprehensibility: God's failure to try gout or toothache on Job.

J
"Je est un autre": et nous?

Judgement: at best and worst, love's non-identical twin.

K
Kindness: not to be despised for its mixed motives.

Knowledge: a growing awareness of ignorance.

L
Love and disrespect: too often conjoined, in the end, at the head as well as the heart.

Love, time and death are the only subjects for poetry, said someone: a three-quarter truth.

M
Melody: a clearing in the jungle.

A mother's death: the final cutting of the umbilical cord.

N
The natural world: how many objects can you think of that you cannot name?

Nature's grandest gesture: the empty horizon.

O

Old age, like childhood, has moments when the fullness of the actual is overwhelming: clouds, the taste of jam, the smell of bacon, the texture of skin, string quartets.

Opera: an amazing construct, a cake of many layers rising in tiers, which somehow – if it works – manages not to fall over, and to reward the taste-buds. But try explaining it to any landing Martian.

P

Politicians: expert trick recyclists.

Punches not pulled: on the Paris Métro, seats marked POUR LES MUTILÉS DE GUERRE.

Q

Questions. For instance: What, do you think, was your moment of greatest understanding? When you discovered the power of words? When you fell in love for the first time? When you realised there was a scent sweeter than the one that lived in your mother's handbag and clung to her skirts? When you first entered the shadow of the valley? When you first wept, on a hot summer night, and caressed your own skin? When it came to you that the frequent caller was neither your father nor your mother's innocent acquaintance?

Quiescence: the move towards the inner wall of truth. But what would be its outer wall?

R

Reversals:

> In an age of reason, Saturday is the unlucky fourteenth.
> In veritate vinum: the sober and intoxicating truth.
> It is more blessed to receive than to give.
> The unpredictable past: the certain future.
> We had the meaning but missed the experience.

Ruthlessness: the most powerful weapon of innocence.

S

Sporting occasions and displays of public grief: two sides of the same coin.

Superstition. A superstitious optimist: someone who always carries a waterproof coat in order to make sure the sun stays out. A superstitious pessimist: someone who always carries a waterproof coat in order to make sure it rains.

T

Time: it runs at you, past you, and you hardly see it coming – or going.

Triumph: the victory of editing over experience.

U

Uncertainty: a saving grace.

Unicorns: if they existed, it would be necessary to uninvent them.

V

Vanity: the attempt to dissociate oneself from Narcissus.

Vulnerability: the shadow side of creative receptivity.

W

Weather: a substitute for conversation.

Wisdom: unlike cleverness, attracts no salary.

X

X in its guises: veto, vote, affection, anti-tank defence, the fate of Andrew, marker of the buried, crossed swords or bones – what other letter so combines impediment and encouragement?

Xenophobia: a failure of hospitality.

Y

Yacht: coracle, skiff, pram, dinghy, lugger, cutter, sloop, yawl, even schooner – none quite rides the waves with the stylishness of a yacht or, quite, with that word's sense of an affirmative cry of exhilaration. What a pity, then, that it also speaks of gladioli on the after-deck, keenly pressed white flannels and cocktails, the houseboats of the rich.

"Yes": assent, but only tone and positioning will tell you what is really being agreed to.

Z

Zero: the moment for action, disguised as nothing.

Zoo: degradation of the peaceable kingdom.

CLOT

It was a dinner party I hadn't known of, following on from a concert to which I'd been taken by London friends. It was smart – sufficiently so to make me feel clumsily under-dressed, rather like Rimbaud arriving in Paris from Charleville. I was assigned to one of a number of small tables, each seating four people: none of my table companions were known to me. The food was a while coming, and already it was obvious that the lady on my right was in her cups: in the delightful disclaimer of the passive Irish locution, drink had been taken. At some point in the conversation, which she was gaily leading, she made a sweeping motion with her arm and knocked over her wine glass, which then knocked over another. As is the way with spilt liquids, a small pool transformed itself into a lake. Chairs were pulled back, the flood was dabbed at with napkins, eager protestations were made about the complete unimportance of the event, the impossibility of the stain not coming out – and when the hostess appeared, clucking with concern for her guest, it was only to cheer her: she was quite sure that the eighteenth-century rosewood table, as she described it, would not be ruined for ever. The tablecloth was replaced, chairs were pulled up, clean napkins brought, glasses refilled and the culprit patted reassuringly. It was all so cheerful that you'd think it was the best thing that could have occurred. Someone may even have said that worse things happen at sea.

A few minutes later she knocked over her glass again.

Appalled stares: silence.

This strikes me as an especially vivid instance of clumsiness, incorporating as it does not only a physical miscalculation but a high degree of ensuing social discomfiture. It was also, presumably, a temporary aberration induced by drink, rather than a natural predisposition. Some people, though, are naturally clumsy, their trail marked by swathes of damage. They have only to turn round to dislodge something and send it crashing to the ground: even such a simple operation as, say, opening a jar of gherkins results inexorably in a vinegary mess of dill, onion, peppercorns and vinegar, with the knobbled fruit rolling across the floor among bright shards of glass. For the naturally clumsy, to inspect a price tag is synonymous with paying for the article in question; to dance, with treading on your partner's foot; stepping out, with missing your footing. Occasionally endearing, such ineptitude more often provokes an irritation fuelled by the tally of damage, or even downright alarm.

Clumsy – the word itself has something going for it, the clanking of buckets as they are inadvertently kicked over. It energetically embodies its meaning in a way entirely absent from the French 'gauche', though 'maladroit' rattles a bit more promisingly. As does the German 'tolpatschig', rather than its more elegant equivalents 'ungeschickt' or 'schwerfällig'. 'Clumsy', from the Middle English *clumsen*, notes the Oxford English Dictionary, 'perhaps of Norse origin' – and with its first meaning 'to be or become numb with cold'. Hence, of course, butter-fingered and more generally awkward.

In any case, more often than not it's a comic shortcoming associated with a lack of grace, or a loss of dignity, denoting a clown who attracts ridicule, mockery, judgement. It keeps the company of 'bungling', 'stumbling', 'botched'. Clumsy fool: from a few decades ago, clumsy *clot*. The embarrassment it can cause may mirror, on the part of those who witness it, anxiety about their own potential for a loss of face: 'there but for the grace of God…'. And there is a peculiar kind of clumsinesss to be seen when people are beginning to perpetrate violence on one another, when they first grapple. By comparison, smoothly staged fights in films, particularly duels, look improbably balletic and elegant, though finally the villain must miss his footing and topple backwards over the cliff edge.

Clumsiness can indeed be lethal, as Félix Fénéon demonstrates all too clearly in his *Novels in Three Lines* (trans. Luc Sante, New York Review Books, 2007). These are tiny newspaper pieces, along the lines of 'News in Brief', many of them not unlike Maupassant stories in miniature. Rich in big implications, they detail mishaps, miscalculations and murders in the year 1906, garnered by Fénéon from the Parisian daily *Le Matin*. Though most chronicle the moments when, in one way or another, enough becomes too much, leading as like as not to a killing, there is also evidence of plain clumsiness. Thus 'M. Abel Bonnard, of Villeneuve-Saint-Georges, who was playing billiards, put out his left eye falling on his cue'. He was marginally luckier than Madame Thévenet, of Maisons-Alfort, who 'knocked over her bedside lamp. Fire consumed the sheets and overtook that 96-year-old person, who succumbed'. Meanwhile, 'In Saint-Cyr, Georges Mahler was fencing with his knife against a lamppost. All he managed to do was cut the artery in his right wrist.'

Things are not always so clear-cut when it comes to considering what clumsiness may portend as a symptom. Anxiety, love, fear, heavy-handedness, a loss of balance brought on by an inner ear infection, the onset of arthritis – any of these might qualify for expression in the body's physical systems, in the guise of clumsiness. It can be symptomatic of certain forms of Parkinson's disease, as well as Alzheimer's, multiple sclerosis and heaven knows what else – the internet has a schedule so long that you feel it would have been simpler to list the few conditions not associated with clumsiness.

Does it get worse with age, as a corollary of preferring one's own bed and always taking bedroom slippers if you do have to go away? Is it part of the brute truth not even to be hidden by a friend's delicate enquiry as to whether God has touched you lightly on the shoulder yet? But the clumsiness of old age is not a single act: rather, it is disseminated and expressed in actions, appearance, gait, gestures, even breathing. Nowhere is it more brilliantly captured than in the stage directions (as much a portrait of the protagonist as dramatic instructions) at the opening of Beckett's short play *Krapp's Last Tape* (1958). Krapp, 'a wearish old man', shows all the marks of age:

> *Disordered grey hair. Unshaven. Very near-sighted (but unspectacled). Hard of hearing. Cracked voice. Distinctive intonation. Laborious walk.*

And the verbs of his world, notably 'peering', 'fumbling' and 'feeling about', are similarly those of a man struggling with the incompetencies of growing old as well as deteriorating eyesight:

> KRAPP ... *heaves a great sigh, looks at his watch, fumbles in his pockets, takes out an envelope, puts it back, takes out a small bunch of keys, raises it to his eyes, chooses a key, gets up and moves to front of table. He stoops, unlocks first drawer, peers into it, feels about inside it, takes out a reel of tape, peers at it, puts it back, locks drawer, unlocks second drawer, peers into it, feels about inside it, takes out a large banana, peers at it, locks drawer, puts key back in his pocket.*

Perhaps worst of all is the clumsiness that the imagination anticipates. You are about to pick up a mug: already the thought of dropping it comes to you. In your mind you see the mug arcing earthwards, almost in slow motion, towards the unforgiving slates of the kitchen floor. Or you envisage catching your foot in the end of the rug, taking a header and being found with a broken leg in the hall of your own house: already you wonder how the paramedics are going to get into the place, seeing that you have left the key in the front door lock. When such prevenient things happen more than once, you can start to wonder whether the idea entering your head won't in fact cause the ensuing damage. Is this a tribute to the lively extrapolations of a brain in good order, or an excuse for the failing body? Best, perhaps, not to enquire too closely: you might trip yourself up.

THE GATEKEEPER

If you look up the name 'Ibrahim Khoury' in the context of the American University of Beirut, you find that he was the director of the Office of Information and Public Relations, and that he retired in October 2009 'after sixteen years of devoted service'. No trace of the different Ibrahim Khoury I got to know a little when in 1962, as an undergraduate, I spent a few days working in the University library, in the course of a summer spent travelling with two friends in Turkey, Syria, Lebanon and Jordan. He was one of the gatekeepers at the main entrance.

Fifty years on, I find him securely lodged in my mind, and more clearly etched than the University itself, of which I remember simply that it had solid and quite old buildings, a spacious airy campus overlooking the Mediterranean, and grounds bright with papery bougainvillaea.

I wonder how we met – most likely I asked the way to the library, and then or later one of us engaged the other in conversation. Quite short in stature, he wore a striped blue shirt of the cheap kind you find in a bazaar or a second-hand clothes stall (sometimes with a famous brand name fraudulently stitched onto the breast pocket), and blue cotton trousers. His shoes didn't quite fit. He had an angular face, black hair, and wore tortoiseshell spectacles. More striking than any of this was a kind of quiet modesty that attached to him, and was somehow made more emphatic by a firmness of speech and an understated dignity. Equable, humorous, it seemed he would be impossible to disconcert. He might have been in his forties.

He told me Khoury was a name peculiar to Arab Christians, denoting that there was or had been a priest in the family, as was indeed the case with him. He intimated that he looked upon the priesthood as his own calling, too, even if circumstances prevented him from fulfilling it. He and his family were Palestinian refugees and, though he never elaborated on his own story, he did suggest that we might visit one of the refugee camps, at Sidon. So we did – and that, too, has left a lasting impression: of remarkable cheerfulness and resilience, of courage, of humour. Of the hospitality that Ibrahim had already shown us and about which we, as Europeans, had yet really to learn. In Lebanon, as in Syria and Jordan, this was not just a matter of welcome and open doors, but a generosity of spirit infinitely richer than any retail acquisition.

I cannot recall whether or not Ibrahim Khoury accompanied us to Sidon, though I think he must have. The most vivid image I retain of our visit there was sitting drinking strong black coffee on a rooftop space, and having the future foretold by an extraordinary, larger than life figure who recalled – without any hint of bitterness, indeed with affection – the British in Palestine. Virtually toothless, wearing a black and white *keffiyeh*, the traditional Arab headdress, he or she (it was hard to tell which) was clad in a long khaki garment which might have been a robe or a long skirt. The news about our future was as simple as the method of divining it: no scapulomancy, or consulting of entrails, just a reading of what the coffee grounds apparently conveyed. The message was straightforward: 'You will meet a beast'. The prospect caused us no anxiety: in fact we didn't even recall it immediately when, a month later, our elderly Land Rover collided with a cow strolling across a Yugoslav *autoput* in early morning fog. A glancing blow, luckily.

A more immediate mishap occurred soon after in Aqaba, where my kitbag with clothes and books was stolen. When I returned to Beirut a week or so later, Ibrahim Khoury it was who took me to buy cheap clothing by way of replacements.

I don't have any memory of saying goodbye to Ibrahim Khoury – and, with the cheerful carelessness of youth, I didn't keep in touch. Did he write an address on a small piece of paper with blue gridlines torn from a notebook?

Now, exactly half a century on, it's the uncertain past that keeps its potency. I think I know what you are doing, Ibrahim Khoury, still squatting in my head even though you have perhaps been dead for some years. You are there not as some sentimental souvenir, but as a measure of all that has not happened to or for you in the years since we met – and of the appalling circumstances that have swirled around you and your people in the way of oppression, civil war, injustice. You deserved better. And who can tell your children's future?

ACKNOWLEDGEMENTS

THE CHALLENGE was first published in *A Room to Live in* (Salt, 2007).

A version of FLIGHTS was included in *The Gist: a celebration of the imagination*, ed. Lindsay Clarke (published by Arvon/ The Write Factor, 2011).

NOTHING TO DECLARE is based on a talk given at the University of Exeter in February 2007.

Paul Klee's TIEF IM WALD is reproduced by kind permission of the Kunstsammlung Nordrhein-Westfalen, Düsseldorf.